We Are...Warrior Queens

Jawahara Saidullah

We are Warrior Queens Copyright © 2024 by Jawahara Saidullah

All rights reserved. No part of this publication may be reproduced, stored in a retrieval system, or transmitted, in any form or by any means without the prior written permission of the author, nor be otherwise circulated in any form of binding or cover other than that in which it is published and without a similar condition being imposed on the subsequent purchaser.

This is a work of fiction. Names, characters, places, and incidents are either the product of the author's imagination or are used fictitiously, and any resemblance to actual persons living or dead, business establishments, events, or locales, is entirely coincidental.

ISBN: 9798878529457

978-1-953100-62-7

Cover design by dreams2media

Editor: Sharona Wilhelm

First Trade Paperback Printing by Scarsdale Publishing, Ltd February 2024

10 9 8 7 6 5 4 3 2

If you purchased this book without a cover, you should be aware that this book is stolen property. It was reposted as "unsold and destroyed" to the publisher, and neither the author nor the publisher has received any payment for this "stripped book."

Trigger Warning

This book depicts scenes of sexual abuse and speaks of self-harm.

For Mira, who made it happen.

Trademark Acknowledgements

Heroines: Powerful Indian Women of Myth and Mystery by
Ira Mukhoty
Raziya Sultan (2011) by R. Gupta
Prozac Nation by Elizabeth Wurtzel
The Ranee of Jhansi by D.V. Tahmankar
Sardhana and its Begum by Father Keegan
Zoom

The warrior queens have haunted my imagination since childhood, and I would not be the person I am without their existence in the world. It's only fair that I thank these remarkable women who helped me dream, who made it normal that women could be fierce and maternal, proud and flawed, selfless and ambitious, and everything in between.

My father Mohammad Saidullah gifted me his sense of rigid integrity and my mother, Qudsiya Saidullah told me stories that helped me transcend my own lived reality. I couldn't have written this book without them. My siblings, Sa'ad, Bano, Lubna and Ahmad; in different and individual ways all four of them helped make me into the person I am today.

I'm lucky to have worked with some remarkable writers who also happen to be my friends. Thank you Paula Read and Katie Hayoz for harassing me and guilting me out of my frequent procrastinations. Sharon Pollack, thank you for believing in me and for your insightful comments and edits. Thank you, Greg Elliott, for your incisive critiques and invaluable comma knowledge. I couldn't have completed this project without you.

Thanks to my husband, Bijoy Sagar, for being my own personal patron of the arts, for putting up with my moods and creating a writing home with me. To my littlest love, Mira, for being my inspiration and for helping me forget what my life was before she came along.

I'd also to thank my publisher Scarsdale Publishing for taking a chance on me based on a Twitter pitch, and for sticking with me despite my many pandemic and life-related delays. A special thanks to Kim Comeau and Sharona Wilhelm at Scarsdale for being kind, understanding and helping me craft this labor of love.

Chapter One

The Emperor and I

"After my death people will realize that none among my children is more worthy to succeed me than my daughter Raziya." Emperor Iltutmush.

Raziya, Emperor of Delhi, 1236-1240

When I was a little girl my much older siblings gave me teasing nicknames: Miss Know-it-all, Chatterbox, Miss Never Wrong. I have an old birthday card with all these monikers written inside. But I don't remember her anymore, that little girl who was unafraid, talkative, and convinced she was always right. By the time I turned nine, I had become quiet, withdrawn, secretive, and even troubled. These changes coincided with the arrival of a man I will call *Iblis*.

Iblis, Arabic for Satan, was created from the smokeless fire by Allah. Ungrateful to his creator, he was cast into hell. Iblis was evil incarnate.

Iblis seemed to loom over me, though now I realize he was not a tall man. I also now know that he was in his thirties, though to me he was and remains timelessly old. He was big with a prosperous, round stomach and a huge dark-black mustache that dominated his large-cheeked face.

He chewed *paan*, betel leaves that stained his lips and mouth blood-red. The hairs of his mustache did not tickle, but were pointy, abrasive wires that poked my skin. He was a trusted family friend, someone my parents had known since his childhood, and he doted on me. When he visited, he would bring me toys my parents wouldn't buy for me and he often whisked me away to get ice cream, sometimes even on school nights.

Just when I grew comfortable with him and looked forward to his visits, the touching, groping, pinching, and squeezing began. He acted as if nothing was wrong and spoke normally to me and to others. Even as his sly, thick fingers crept up my plump little-girl thighs into my flowered, cotton underwear when I sat on his lap, he joked with my mother, asked the servant for more tea, and questioned me about school. His casual manner made me wonder if I was imagining things, whether anything bad was really happening. If he was doing something wrong, how could he do it with other people around? I must be imagining things, awful things.

As an adult, I now understand I was being gaslit by an expert. He made me question my recollections, doubt my experiences, so that I would assume his guilt as my own. When he committed these despicable acts, I was alone and lonely. My much older protective siblings had all moved away from home by then, so I was essentially an only child in an adult world. The only recourse was to retreat within my self-created shell.

Chapter One

By age ten, I hated what he did to me. I often wished he would have an accident on the way to our house, his body smashed and bloodied on the road. Then a wave of guilt would swallow me. What kind of person was I to wish these horrors on someone who had been so nice to me? Had he been nice?

How could I tell anyone what he was doing to me when I couldn't figure out whether it was right or wrong? Was what he did to me really wrong or was I just a naughty girl with too much imagination and a dirty mind? What if I told my parents and he accused me of lying? Would they believe him?

My parents were old-school, firm in their belief that children often made up stories, and adults were inherently more trustworthy. Respect for my elders was an ingrained value passed down through the generations. On the one hand, this tradition ensured that all of us siblings treated our elders with respect, including servants and anyone in the service industries. This built in respect for my elders programmed me to obey grownups without question.

Iblis was a powerful politician, which made him a good friend to maintain. I was just a child known for being naughty. As a young girl, I already had the reputation for lying when the neighbors accused me and my neighborhood friends of stealing guavas or mangoes from their trees. I often got my much older siblings into trouble by exaggerating their misdeeds. Why would I be believed now?

At eleven, I was close to the age Iblis had been when my mother first met him. As a shy, new bride of twenty-one, alone in India, she missed her five younger siblings she'd left behind in Rangoon. Iblis was the orphaned little brother-in-law of a neighbor, who was raising him as his own. The neighbor was a colleague of my father in the Indian administrative Service (IAS) and a respected family friend. My mother bonded with Iblis, and he became a surrogate for her younger brothers. These long-term ties of family, tradition, friendship, and respect greatly contributed to muting my voice.

Though Iblis lived in a small town quite a distance away, he began visiting us regularly because of a legal matter pending at the state High Court in my hometown, *Allahabad*. My mother always delighted in seeing him and treated him with affectionate indulgence. My father, oblivious to anything not blatantly on the surface, loved to discuss politics with Iblis. Their talk of court proceedings and common friends further isolated me, as their connection pre-dated my existence.

I had no language, no vocabulary to describe what was happening. I also lacked the conceptual framework to make sense of my experiences enough to be able to vocalize them. I escaped to the only place I could: within myself. I perfected the emotionless, impassive face that frustrates those around me even now. No one could or would ever know what I was thinking, feeling, or experiencing. I was my own refuge. I needed no one.

Yet, the hidden tender part of me knew I needed protection and that I should fight. To do that, I needed to be someone else. Someone unafraid, someone with power, someone with a voice who knew the right words and who to say them to, in order to stop him. I didn't have the language to form even these thoughts, but I recognized them through the images and fragments swirling in my childish brain.

These forces encircled me, arranged with military precision by Iblis. Dealing with him as a child and with the toxic memories he created became my battleground. Ultimately, the instinct to retreat and escape was my salvation. I learned to disappear through the backdoor when I knew he was to visit, or if I heard his voice calling out a greeting to my parents when he entered the front door.

At thirteen, I remember listening to my father and a fellow history buff friend discuss the reign of Raziya Sultan. The discussion was not about her gender but about whether she lived up to her father's ambitions for her. I don't remember the details of the conversation, but the name and the concept of a female emperor stuck with me. I remember how when defeat was certain, she re-strategized to fight again.

That's what I did. I chose retreat because allowing Iblis to continue the abuse was inconceivable. I recognized the distinctive, loud, sputtering of his Vespa scooter. Silently, I would head to the backdoor, flatten myself against the wall and peer down the dimly lit hallway into the living room and beyond to the front door. It was easy to be a spy in my century-old sprawling Indian house with each doorway and window aligned with the next for efficient cross-ventilation. I had a clear view of the entrance and held my breath as the edge of the door swung open and he exchanged pleasantries with the servant who granted him entrance.

I didn't wait for even a glimpse of the blinding white of the crisp cotton of his *kurta-pyjama*, but raced out the back door before he could see me. I hurried to the servants' quarters where I had friends and spent my hard-won escape playing hopscotch.

Gaining the courage to escape his molestations was my first act of agency bestowed upon me when I first learned about Raziya Sultan. Like her, I took charge of my destiny. Over the next couple years, I perfected excuses for my absence and selected several hiding places, and so managed to never be alone with him again.

As I filled my imagination with all I could read about

Raziya and went on with my life, traumatic memories slipped away like water. I didn't deliberately erase Iblis, but the recollections became hazily indistinct, as if I were an observer with no emotional connection. Of course, I now understand this is a survival tactic. At the time, however, I went on with my life. A single day at a time, a single task at a time, one foot in front of the other. My memories of Iblis receded behind a gauze curtain, behind a sign that said, Do Not Enter.

I truly discovered Raziya in the pages of my medieval history textbook in sixth grade. I read and reread every sparse detail about her. Like me, she was closer to her father than her mother. Like me, she wanted to be like him. Like me, she never wanted to be a victim despite being victimized.

Raziya was the only female Muslim Emperor in the world and the only Muslim woman to ever sit on the throne of Delhi, the most powerful and largest kingdom in medieval India. The two frustratingly short paragraphs about her in my textbook left me wanting more. However, for a figure of truly historic proportions there was not much more to be found.

Despite the centuries that separated Raziya and I, like me, she was a North-Indian Muslim woman. Many women of importance presented to me as role-models—some of them Muslim—were holier-than-thou, self-sacrificing, virtuous, uninspiring paragons. My middle name itself is testament to these types of women: Khadija, the first wife of the prophet Mohammad, the first convert to Islam. She was a widow and businesswoman who proposed to her young employee and married him. Then she became the ideal wife, understanding, supportive and gentle, peerless among women. And therefore, to me, utterly boring.

While other little girls dreamed of finding the perfect man, I dreamed of being a warrior queen. Raziya was my role-model, the antithesis of everything young girls from nice

Chapter One

Indian Muslim families should aspire to be. Raziya was unmarried, child-free, blunt, forthright, and strong, the center of her own universe. Her legacy—like most men of her era—is measured by what she did and not how she looked or how well she kept house. When I think of Raziya, my imagination fills in the gaps history omits.

The young Princess Raziya was not only unique herself but was descended from a unique family. Her father, the Emperor Iltutmush, was a slave or a Mamluk (owned) who was sold off by jealous family members to settle scores against his family. He was bought by the marauding Muhammad Ghori in a Central Asian slave market and was later re-sold to the Emperor Qutub-ud-din-Aibak, the monarch of Delhi.

Despite the fact that Iltutmush was a slave, Emperor Aibak was so impressed by him that he made him governor of a province. Being a slave did not condemn Raziya's father to a life of servitude. A Mamluk could become a trusted confidant or more. Once he broke all bonds of his former life, the Mamluk could be indoctrinated into his master's image. The process was brainwashing of sorts. The slave became a part of his master, identifying with his master and implicitly trusted. Once loyalty was assured, some of these capable men often took the place of favorite sons. Iltutmush rose to prominence through his own merit and accomplishments before seizing power. Like his daughter one day would.

Perhaps his own history taught Iltutmush that being a woman did not invalidate his daughter from succeeding him. Upon Aibak's death, his son Aram Shah ascended the throne, but was widely decried as an unfit ruler. With the approval and help of the Turkish nobility, Iltutmush took over as Sultanate of Delhi. In medieval Indian history, this is known as the age of the Slave Dynasty. During his reign, the kingdom of Delhi spanned about one thousand miles, roughly the size of the state of Colorado and larger than the modern country of Portugal.

Iltutmush's son and heir, Nasiruddin Mahmud, died suddenly in 1229. The emperor turned to his daughter—strangely enough still unmarried in her twenties—and gave her administrative responsibilities. This made use of her education in statecraft and her skills in war.

In 1231, to the shock of his conservative courtiers, he formally declared her his heir, choosing her over his two other sons. When they asked for a justification for this unusual choice he said, "My sons are devoted to the pleasures of youth, and not one of them is qualified to be king. They are unfit to rule the country, and after my death you will find that there is no one more competent to guide the State than my daughter."

That same year, in an unprecedented move, Iltutmush left Raziya, his newly named heir, to rule in his place as he led his army to quell rebellions in a far-flung area of the kingdom. There are no accounts of how she felt, of course, though she validated her father's trust by being a capable administrator in his absence for the two years Iltutmush was away. Surely, she was aware of the stakes. Growing up as she had in court, she knew all-too-well of the treachery and dangers lying in wait for her.

In July 2012, I arrived in Raziya's Delhi, miles from the current city. That year was one of the city's hottest, driest summers, with temperatures of around forty-two degrees Celsius (108 Fahrenheit). As I stepped from the air-conditioned car, the intense dry heat evaporated my sweat almost before it rose to the surface of my skin. My ice-cold bottle of water became lukewarm within minutes.

The kingdom of Delhi was destroyed and re-built seven

times. Each invader, each Central Asian marauder, targeted this ancient city. Successive dynasties ruled India but Delhi, long the seat of power, was captured only once. The outlines of Delhi were amorphous because of its constantly shifting borders. Where one ruler placed his or her capital was often not where another might. In contemporary Delhi, buildings from various eras of history coexist, from prehistoric Patliputra through the Lodis, Mughals, British, independent Indian, and others in between.

Raziya's capital existed in what is now the suburb of Mehrauli, a few miles from New Delhi. Referred to as the Qutub complex, her capital was the seat of Mamluk power and that of Qutub-ud-din-Aibak.

The complex spans hundreds of acres, and is studded with seventy structures, many in ruins. Dusty trails connect the monuments. Above them all, soars the Qutub Minar, once the tallest structure in Asia at nearly two hundred and ninety-three feet. It is still the tallest brick minaret in the world.

On this hot day, far fewer tourists were visiting than normal. Annually, the ancient capital draws more tourist traffic than the Taj Mahal in Agra. I meandered among the sparse crowd as I entered the seat of Raziya's power.

To one side of the Qutub Minar stands the Quwwat-ul-Islam—the supremacy of Islam—mosque that proclaims the triumph of the faith of the Islamic conquerors built over the indigenous Hindu temple that once stood there. The mosque sits upon a vast platform of stone that traps and magnifies the temperature.

I hurried to escape the searing heat of the burning stone through my thin-soled sandals and entered the relative coolness of the Quwwat-ul-Islam Mosque. I stepped down into the interior and relished the cooling relief of the uneven flagstones on the soles of my feet.

I traced a finger along the stone pillars as I walked. This structure had been built upon the remains of twenty-seven Jain and Hindu temples. Building upon the remains of a vanquished enemy was a fairly common practice even among warring Hindu kingdoms. This secured ready-made materials and crowned the conqueror's victory.

For Muslim invaders, destroying temples and using their debris asserted their supremacy. To adhere to the Islamic prohibition of recreating the human form and its strictures against idol worship, faces of humans and gods were chiseled off the pillars and walls. My fingers dipped into the one particularly rough divot that had once been the lovingly sculpted face of a celestial beauty. Destruction and violence: the enduring legacies of empire.

Though I was grown, Raziya Sultan remained a childish caricature, created as my champion. Now, as I entered her domain, I saw more of her complexities. She had been an ambitious woman who pitted herself against orthodox, dark forces. She was daughter, schemer, at once ruthless and seductive, powerful, a wife, a lover...and emperor. She belonged to a harsher time and was part of a culture that valorized destruction. I reminded myself that I too was a product of my time.

The sunbaked trails cut through tall green grass swaying in the wind and trees. I could scarcely believe that I now walked the very place where Raziya proclaimed herself Sultan and ascended the throne of Delhi. She refused to take the titles Sultana or Empress because they were titles of a mere consort, devoid of true power. She considered herself the source and the center of royal power.

Like Pharaoh Hatshepsut of the 18th Dynasty in Egypt around 1470 BC, Raziya too made her gender a non-issue. She was Emperor. That she was a woman was immaterial, at least to her. By the power of her personality and her royal status, she ensured that others didn't care she was a woman. At least until they did.

How did that happen? Daughters, especially during her time eight hundred years ago, lived in royal seclusion with their mothers until they were married off for useful strategic political alliances. However, in Raziya's case, her father ordered that, like her three brothers, she should be trained in the martial arts. She learned to ride a horse, to fight, and she became proficient with weapons and learned the strategies of warfare and diplomacy. I wonder why her father made this fateful decision. Perhaps he saw something exceptional in his daughter and perhaps he, like his daughter, was a man out of time.

I was born into a believing yet lax Muslim household. That essentially meant we abstained from alcohol and pork but didn't pray five times a day. We followed the traditions of North-Indian Islam and learned to read the Quran in Arabic and celebrated the two major Muslim holidays of Eid-ul-Fitr and Eid-ul-Zuha. Yet, despite the rather conservative Indian town we lived in, we never wore a veil. We went to a Catholic convent school and wore jeans and t-shirts. On my mother's side of the family, her grandmother was the last woman to wear a burqa. My father had four female cousins. The youngest two were named Raziya and Sultana. While more observant Muslims than us, they had PhD and M.A. degrees, worked outside the home, and came and went freely.

The freedoms of life, freedom of passage, interacting with males, education and exposure to the outside world were Raziya's only because her powerful father allowed those freedoms. The freedoms I took for granted were mine only because my parents allowed them. I know many parents who still hold back their daughters from living self-determined, full lives.

I looked at the landscape that Raziya had certainly gazed upon. As I walked where I imagined Raziya had walked, I kept in mind her and my legacy. Despite my fascination with her and my debt to her, she had always remained elusive, unknown, faceless, not truly real.

The haphazard collection of buildings included another small mosque, a handful of mausoleums, the remains of a smaller minaret meant to rival the Qutub Minar, as well as living quarters. Other structures had been built during the reign of the Mamluks, along with those constructed before and after the decline of the Slave dynasty.

The structures here were simple compared to the grand ornate structures built by subsequent rulers of Delhi like those in the Mehrauli suburbs. These buildings were utilitarian, practical, unembellished as befits warrior kings and queens who sat on uncertain, newly created thrones. Their efforts were focused on retaining power not on creating magnificent legacies in stone. They left that to the Lodis, Mughals, and British.

Historical sources and academic writings on Raziya are few and far between. She appears in the few books written about female warriors and is the main character in the historical novel, *Raziya Sultan (2011) by R. Gupta*, in which Raziya returns to contemporary Delhi where she laments the city's changes.

No official portraits of her survived. Those who deposed her and made certain her grave was never found almost certainly intended to erase her from history. The only mental picture I have of her is a simple line-drawn picture in my schoolbooks derived from her likeness on the coins she minted during her reign. Before seeing that crude portrait, I always imagined her as someone who looked like me, the quintessential, north-Indian Muslim with a mélange of diverse races, from Turks to Central Asian tribes and Mongols, and from Arabs to the native-born Hindu merchants.

Even now, I see her as that line drawing or, as I prefer, as my doppelgänger. I can superimpose my own face within the outlines of her crude portrait. I can become her and make her part of me. But I am no longer a child searching for a strong alter ego. As I walked where she did, I tried to imagine Raziya as she might have been.

I see her in the image of her Turkish forbears, as does Ira Mukhoty in her 2017 book, *Heroines: Powerful Indian Women of Myth and Mystery*. Raziya is described as having, "high cheekbones, wind-blown complexion and almond eyes characteristic of the people of the Steppes."

Some of my features carry the stamp of those Central Asian invaders. I look uncannily like my father and his father before him, round face, big cheeks that feature high cheekbones, a blunt short nose and small, almond-shaped, dark brown eyes characteristic of Central Asians.

I used to joke with my dad about being related to the great Mongol warrior, Genghis Khan or rather about being descended from one of his less ambitious foot soldiers. It became less of a joke once I learned that sixteen million men —or one in two hundred men—in the world, mostly in Asia, bear genetic traces of Genghis Khan's DNA (The National Geographic, 2003). Perhaps the intertwined strands of my DNA brushed against one of Raziya's. The odds are much greater than I once thought. I amuse myself by imagining a link between Raziya and me. This fantasy is safe, as it can never be tested because of the mystery that surrounds the fate of her body.

Despite Iltutmush's directive that Raziya was his heir, after his death in 1236, the nobles placed his second son, Rukn-uddin, on the throne. His powerful mother, Shah Turkan, Iltutmush's concubine, supported him. Intent on avenging real or imagined slights from other members of the royal harem, she had her rivals murdered and settled old scores with enemies. She also engineered the decimation of the young prince, her stepson Kutub-uddin by having him blinded then put to death.

Within months of the ascension, the new Sultan Rukn-uddin faced revolts from various quarters, including some powerful nobles. He was reputed to be out of touch with his people and seemed blissfully unaware of how his misrule affected the common people. The people increasingly looked to Raziya as the true heir to the throne, which did not go unnoticed by Rukn-uddin's mother.

While he was away quelling rebellions in other parts of the empire, Shah Turkan plotted to assassinate Raziya. By the time Sultan Rukn-uddin returned from these military campaigns, an attempt had been made on Raziya's life. The princess, having learned of the plot, used the opportunity to thrust herself into the limelight, simultaneously saving her life and seizing the throne.

Lightly-veiled and dressed in white—the color of the wronged and aggrieved—Raziya presented herself to the army, which remained loyal to the memory of her father. Crowds of people—many of whom supported her— clustered together for this unparalleled event.

She ran up to the palace rooftop, looked down upon the crowd, and proclaimed, "My brother killed his brother, and he now wants to kill me." Aligning herself with the memory of her father, she insisted on justice from the men he had once commanded. She demanded their loyalty as her due. Raziya knew her worth. She knew what she wanted, and she wasn't shy about staking her claim as his legitimate successor.

The army and the assembled crowds were so moved that they stormed the palace and captured Rukn-uddin, then brought him to Raziya.

"The slayer shall be slain," she proclaimed.

And so, it was done.

The jubilant crowd carried Raziya on their shoulders to the throne and sat her upon it. She proclaimed herself Sultan Raziya bint Iltutmush or Emperor Raziya, daughter of Iltutmush in the same manner as male emperors had always been crowned. In doing so, she imbued herself with legitimacy, legacy, and power.

Shah Turkan, once the terror of the harem and the insidious power behind her son Rukn-uddin, was also captured. Though Shah Turkan's fate remains a mystery, there can be no doubt her death was unpleasant and violent. Like other rulers of her time, Raziya was ruthless, cruel even, intent on retaining what she considered hers. To solidify her position, enemies, even if they were within her family circle, had to be neutralized. She lived in ruthless, violent times and had to be the same, in order to survive and thrive.

My enemy, however, lived within. Unexpected flashes of forgotten memories kept me off-kilter and unable to fight. Therapy was a series of battles that made up a long war I feared I was losing.

I attended classes and seminars, taught two undergraduate public speaking courses, and tried to pretend all was well. I focused on one day at a time for fear that these memories would roll over me like a tsunami.

These were the battles I fought: I had to let go of my own guilt, forgive myself, put the blame where it belonged—squarely with Iblis. This would be a life-long campaign to resist weakness during which the toxicity that bubbled up made me punish myself. My self-punishment took many forms; self-sabotage, selling myself short, a lack of belief in myself and my abilities, dark, malevolent thoughts that swirled inside me.

The only thing that made me feel better, that let me drain away the poison at least for a while was cutting. Ah, the utter banality of cutting. I held it like a talisman within me, not recognizing the action for the addiction it was. Ultimately, cutting was about control of my own body, albeit in a twisted way. The nick of pain reminded me I was alive. The flow of blood momentarily eased the tension. Healed scars reminded me that, if nothing else, I had this.

Years later, in 1994, as a depressed twenty-seven-year-old newlywed, I read the just published *Prozac Nation* by Elizabeth Wurtzel. Until I read of Wurtzel's cutting behavior, I never considered the possibility that others might be doing what I considered to be my dirty little secret. Later, I realized that cutting was commonplace enough to be boring, mostly the domain of angsty teens. It was my angry addiction, and I was well into my early thirties before I stopped using cutting as a coping mechanism.

My journey was far from over but, thankfully, slowly but surely, I began to develop a sense of self. Just as Raziya developed as a ruler. She gained confidence and became more martial. She had already discarded her light veil as an inconvenience and started wearing men's clothes. She rode upon her elephant by herself in public areas, allowing the populace to openly view their monarch, as was their right. By taking on the attributes of traditional male monarchs, she blurred gender lines and imbued herself with some of the privilege that came with being a man. She even minted coins with her name and image on them.

These unorthodox actions made her many enemies among the conservative noblemen and religious leaders. She threatened their power and influence. The Muslim clergy started plotting afresh against the humiliation and heresy of being ruled by a woman.

In the 1980's while young American girls and women were becoming enthralled with power suits and the intoxicating pull of modern feminism, I idolized Raziya. For me, she had the glamorous appeal of a comic-book superhero. She gave young girls permission to have an ego and to put themselves first. She was far removed from Indian and Muslim female role-models who were self-effacing, self-sacrificing, modest, chaste, and virtuous. In other words, boring. Imagining myself as an adventurer answerable to no one kept me from wandering into the areas of my mind where lay the hidden memories. Raziya lent me a sense of power and the knowledge that girls with ego and pride could make their own destiny.

Despite Raziya's inspiration, I drifted. Like a girl trapped in amber, I did what needed to be done. School. Studies. National board exams. I didn't fail but I wasn't the best. I coasted, always outside real life. Quiet and withdrawn, I became adept at disappearing into any background. My teens merged into my twenties, and I remained the same, though to an outsider, the trajectory of my life appeared to be upward. High school graduation, college, graduate school, and a teaching assistantship in the U.S.

I was twenty-two, and in my second semester of graduate school of Communications at the University of Kentucky. Yellow-gold and red leaves of autumn swirled in the wind-tunnel created by the tall building of the main quad. Huddled in my winter jacket, I hurried along the walkway.

I don't remember where I was headed or for what reason.

I don't even remember what I was thinking or feeling. I only remember being startled by my reflection in the tinted windows of the Patterson building. Black streaks of mascara and eyeliner running down my face made me look like a sad clown. My fingers came away wet when I touched my cheeks. I looked up at the blue, cloudless sky, puzzled. I hurried inside the building and to the bathroom.

I hovered outside myself, looking in the mirror at my red-rimmed eyes and even redder nose. How long had I been crying? Why was I crying? Why hadn't I noticed? I knew this wasn't normal. A few days earlier, I had seen a flyer publicizing counseling services for students. I had given the flyer no thought. Now I reached toward the help as a lifeline. It was either that or death.

In her twenties, Raziya faced more tangible, bigger and pressing issues than those I faced in the sudden flood of clear and noxious memories of Iblis. In my early and mid-twenties, I headed to therapy to deal with buried trauma, whereas, Raziya had learned statecraft. She was learning to rule, readying herself to shoulder the burden of being Emperor.

I thought of her as I tried to moderate and make sense of memories that I had worked so hard to suppress. One of the lessons of statecraft that helped Raziya survive as long as she did was to limit her trust to a very few people. I learned this lesson too late because as a child I lacked the agency to make decisions to avoid people like Iblis. It was also a lesson that eventually swung in the opposite direction, a lesson I had to unlearn: trust no one. Let no one in. This lesson turned out to be imperative for Raziya's survival as well.

Despite the walls I had so carefully constructed around myself, love found a way, as it is wont to do. It was dizzying, falling into this abyss with eyes closed. My future husband and I got to know each other through our typed words on old-fashioned, text-only socio-political bulletin boards. This was the internet before the web, in late 1991.

Soon, we were talking on the phone for hours. He lived in another state and visited me in 1993. That was it. A few months later, around March of 1994, he moved to Kentucky for a new job. On July 31, 1994, we impulsively decided to get married. We got married fifteen days later, on August 15, 1994. I knew this new relationship might destroy my familial bonds. Still, I couldn't stop myself. I never wavered.

We faced one huge complication; I was a Muslim woman
—albeit lapsed—
married to a Hindu man. There were few things more scandalous to both communities, even thousands of miles away from India. Our union was analogous to an inter-racial marriage of the 1950s deep south in the U.S. In many Indian villages and among poorer sections of society, a union such as this can still lead to honor killings. My parents, who had never worn their religion on their sleeves, suddenly quoted the Quran, telling me that our marriage would never be valid in Allah's eyes.

My father, whose genetic markers I saw reflected in my own features and whom I hero-worshipped, wrote me a letter. I remember nothing else from that letter except the words: *"You have betrayed and hurt me as I could never imagine. You are dead to me. Consider me dead to you."*

I felt unmoored from my life, from my past and my family, from myself. Teetering on the edge of one of the deepest depressions of my life, I fell into a bottomless crevasse.

Raziya too had been in love—or rumored to have been—with the wrong kind of man, her Ethiopian master of the stables, Amir Jamal-uddin Yakut. Despite being an emperor, she was still a thirteenth century Muslim woman and just the impression of impropriety left her vulnerable to attack. This was the opening her enemies had so patiently waited for. The clerics and Turkish nobles smeared her character with vicious rumors. It is unclear whether the Sultan and employee were romantically involved. The smoking gun used against her was that she often leaned on Yakut while he helped her mount her horse.

For a woman, to let a man touch her openly in this way was scandalous. She was an emperor. He was a mere employee. Since he felt free enough to take the liberty of touching her in public, that had to mean they were having an affair. A new barrage of rebellions started against her. Her enemies now had a moral and religious impetus.

The rebel leader, Nur-uddin Turk struck the first blow. The plot came to fruition on a Friday, the Islamic sabbath, when religious Muslims gather for prayers at mosques. On March 1237 AD, about a thousand armed rebels stormed the crowded main mosque. Many people were killed by the sword-bearing rebels while some died in the panicked stampede. The coup was unsuccessful however, because warriors loyal to the Sultan Raziya rode into the mosque, fully armed and ready for battle. They slaughtered most of the rebels while the townsfolk who had fled to the rooftop for refuge pelted the intruders with rocks and stones.

The conspiracies and rebellions didn't stop. One revolt was led by the nobles, Kabir Khan-i-Ayaz, and Malik Izz-uddin. They gathered against her at the gates of Delhi and the opposing armies squared off and laid siege to the capital. The feudal lord of Awadh marched to her aid but as he crossed the Ganga, the Maliks took him captive. Already suffering from some ailment, the man soon died as a prisoner.

The siege continued, until Raziya established camp on the banks of the Jamuna and fought several pitched battles with the insurgents. Some of the rebels switched allegiance to her and together they conspired to summon the leaders of the rebellion to her presence to capture and imprison them. However, the targets learned of the plot and fled. Raziya gave chase and killed or imprisoned those she caught.

The thrill of victory was short-lived. In 1239 AD the feudatory of Lahore declared a revolt against the Sultan. Raziya Sultan led her army in pursuit of her enemy and ruthlessly put down the rebellion. Secretly abetted by other nobles. the powerful Malik Ikhtiyar-uddin Altunia launched the next revolt in the region of Tabarhindah.

When the sultan rode out to confront Altunia, the Turkish nobles treacherously rose against her, killed Yakut, and imprisoned her. These powerful nobles placed her half-brother Muiz-ud-din Bahram Shah on the throne.

I wonder how Raziya—the woman—felt? Yakut, even if not her lover, was certainly a trusted ally and confidant, maybe even a friend. After witnessing his violent death, she found herself alone in prison with no one to trust, no one in her corner. She was isolated and in grave danger.

I remember the feeling of isolation and the feeling of being alone. As my new husband and I traversed the first years of marriage, we moved across the country for work, first to Virginia, then briefly to California, I lost my parents. Not to death, but to what can only be described as a shunning. My siblings and I still communicated, and they were supportive. However, I felt the loss of my father most keenly. I was his favorite child, the only one not afraid of him, who could cut through his usual stern visage to make him laugh. Even though I knew I had done nothing wrong, I felt guilty about what he perceived to be a betrayal. But I, at least, had someone I loved and who loved me; my husband.

Trapped as Raziya was in enemy territory, however, she had no one. Surely, she must have grieved and railed against her ills. She must have longed for someone she could trust. Eventually, the rebel nobles grew tired of Sultan Bahram's opulent living and started to resent his power. They hatched a plot to assassinate him. Raziya remained in captivity, biding her time, and making plans. She also found someone—a most unlikely someone—to trust and perhaps, even to love: her captor and enemy, Altunia.

Whether due to love or opportunism, the two grew close. Some accounts say they had been childhood sweethearts, but there is no compelling evidence to support this claim. In 1240 AD, captor and captive were married. Altunia pledged his fealty to Raziya as his sovereign and became her political and military ally. The marital bond ensured his loyalty to her. The couple focused upon winning back the deposed Sultan's realm now that Altunia's strong army was hers to command.

The newlyweds marched at the head of their combined army toward Delhi. They were soon joined by other nobles, aligned against the emperor, Bahram Shah, who headed his own massive army. In a double-cross, rebel troops soon deserted the Bahram Shah's army to support Raziya. Perhaps Raziya felt unstoppable for she had defeated Bahram Shah. Now she only needed to sit on the throne and rule once more. She could taste victory.

However, Raziya and Altunia's success was short-lived, for when they arrived at Kaithal they encountered hostile forces. Altunia was killed in battle. Raziya was again bereaved, alone, and on the run.

The famous Moroccan traveler Ibn Batata wrote about what happened next, using eyewitnesses accounts. Ibn Batuta writes that Raziya escaped from the battlefield after her army's defeat and Altunia's death. Dressed as a man as she always did, she was famished and exhausted. She came upon a farmer and begged for food. He gave her bread and, after eating, the exhausted Raziya fell asleep. As she slept, the farmer glimpsed her inner garment, a tunic trimmed in gold and pearls. He murdered her, stripped her off her valuables and buried her body in an unmarked grave. What an ignoble death of an emperor.

When the farmer tried to sell the jewels, suspicious dealers took him before the local magistrate, whereupon he confessed to the murder. The dead Sultan's body was exhumed by those loyal to her, bathed according to custom, and wrapped in a proper funeral shroud before being properly buried, according to Ibn Batuta, on the banks of the Yamuna. However, the location pin pointed by Ibn Batuta might lack veracity for the tomb he identified as hers is only one of three sites that claim to be her final resting place. To date, none of the three have been confirmed to be her grave.

The date of her death is accepted to be October 13, 1240 AD. She was just thirty-five years old and had been emperor for three years, six months and six days.

On a muggy, hot yet overcast day I visited the dilapidated black marble tomb in Old Delhi long rumored to be Raziya's final resting place. The tomb is a crumbling ruin within a dilapidated courtyard, surrounded by overgrown, knee-high weeds and wild grass. A slightly askew metal sign in English and Urdu proclaims the tomb to be the supposed burial site of Emperor Raziya. A few months after my visit, the Archaeological Department of India declared that this tomb belonged to a Sufi saint and not to the female Sultan. There is still no proof of where she might have been laid to rest.

Perhaps that quest is fruitless. Raziya lived her life in the present and the future. She sought power, exercised power, then lost that power, only to spend the remainder of her short life trying to get it back. That was the mission, and the focus of her life, so does it really matter where she is buried? Why should she be defined by how she died instead of how she lived? Without concrete evidence of a verified grave, she transcends mere human ambition and greatness and, perhaps in some sense, she never truly died.

To me, her spirit is vital and universal and alive in every woman who challenges the establishment and takes what is rightfully hers. That is Sultan Raziya's true legacy. I felt her presence keenly in the Qutub complex, her seat of power. I stood beside the marble cenotaph of her father Iltutmush, placed within a courtyard of ornately carved red sandstone. I ran my fingers over the smooth surface of the tomb. This is the majesty and grandeur of an emperor's grave. I thought of his daughter in an unmarked grave, never to be honored for the exceptional woman she was.

Only recently have the kingdoms of Europe decreed that the first-born child—not the first-born son—could sit on the throne. Yet, six hundred years ago, a visionary Indian Muslim king—who was once a slave—defied the conventions of his time and raised a female warrior who would become Emperor.

Despite the crowds thronging the complex, I was alone in the peaceful courtyard. I felt strangely connected with this place, almost as if Iltutmush's daughter lay beside him in the royal tomb. Though I lost my faith long ago, something compelled me to cover my head with my dupatta, close my eyes, and haltingly whisper the *fateha*, the prayer for the dead.

O Allah, forgive Raziya and elevate her station among those who are guided. Send her along the path of those who came before and forgive us and her. O Lord of the worlds, enlarge her grave for her comfort and shed light in it for her.

Indian Muslims recite this prayer at the graves of loved ones or strangers for the peace of the departed. Conservative traditional Muslims, especially those from the Middle East, consider this heresy, for once people are dead and buried, they are gone forever and beyond the power of prayer. I had never before recited the fateha and I felt no celestial benediction as I said it that day. I did, however, feel the presence of Sultan Raziya, like a sigh of reprieve. Slipped in between the strong, hot slaps of wind wafted a momentary down-draft of coolness. I lifted my face to enjoy the breeze, but it faded away too quickly.

In 1996, I lived in Indianapolis. My father visited Kentucky that year and, to my surprise, he sent me a message through my mother. He had been in the States for four months. This would be his last week here and he wanted to see me. My husband and I drove the five hours to Kentucky, and I saw him in that familiar crisp white, *kurta pajama*. As a child, I used to snuggle up next to him and run my finger against the sharp fused edge of the cloth on his sleeve until I fell asleep. I looked at him and I was once again six years old before my world had been violated. I was, at last, home again.

He made no recriminations, no complaints, no postmortems. That was my father, once he decided or said something, it was done. He had chosen a relationship with me over his religion. My husband took him out for coffee and upon their return my father declared himself satisfied that I had married a good man. Then he went into the bedroom and returned with one of his favorite ties—he loved ties and had a trunkful of them—and gave it to my husband. My fractured family had started to heal.

One evening in 1998, my mother called. I had a strained, almost formal relationship with her. I, like my siblings, did not trust her with emotions or secrets for she was wont to use them against us. I always had my walls up against her.

We chit-chatted about nothing at all—gossip from back

home mostly—then, just in passing, she gave me the news. Iblis was dead of a sudden heart attack. As I processed the information she continued talking—as if this was just anyone's death—how his family was mourning, who went to the funeral, and on and on.

I laughed. "Good, I'm so glad."

Silence. Then, "How can you say that? He had a young daughter."

"I'm sure she's happy too. Who knows what he must have done to her?"

This was quintessentially my mother, entirely oblivious to the emotions of others. To her, what happened was in the past, erased. In my twenties, I told her about the molestations. She was shocked and asked why I hadn't told her. How could I have not told her? Why didn't I tell her? Why had I done that to *her*?

"This is why," I had screamed. "Because everything becomes about you. Nothing happened to you. It happened to me because you forced me to be with that man. And you let me know...let us all know...that our word would never be believed against an adult. I couldn't tell you because I didn't know how. You never wondered why I always found a way to escape his presence? Why I gave up ice cream and toys rather than go with him? No. You told me I was being rude, to be a good girl, to not embarrass you. What was I going to tell you even if I had had the language to tell you?"

That was the most honest I had ever been with my mother and for a while she seemed to get it, to really get it. Then her etch-a-sketch mind reverted back to the proprieties of behavior. My refusal to forgive and forget in the wake of Ilbis's untimely death, not to mention my pleasure, was an insult to death itself, perhaps even to God. She pointed out that I had a happy life, things had worked out for me and, frankly, it was just unseemly to hold a grudge for so long.

I didn't care. Satan was dead. Life seemed brighter.

This is where Raziya and I diverged. I survived my enemy. She did not. Though I had nothing to do with Iblis's death I had fantasized about it often. I won my battle simply by being alive while he became worm food. I still felt no regret for my reaction to his death. Even now, I feel only relief and satisfaction at his fate.

Raziya's ultimate enemy was her lust and that of others around her. She had been a sultan, commander of armies, ruler of men. Who could turn their back on that? How could she not fight or die trying? Anything less would be a half-life. She understood the stakes.

I rested my palm on the smoothly worn stone lintel and connected with the earth, with this place where Raziya had lived and ruled. I thanked her for being my inspiration during dark times, for showing me that even when defeat is certain it is best to fight, for giving me the courage to face my demons and emerge from the terror and darkness. In that moment, I felt the warmth of the stone as if it were a living thing that linked me to the past and the doomed emperor with whom I had always felt a kinship.

Silently, I said goodbye.

Amir Khusro, a famous Sufi poet born a half century after Raziya sat on the throne of Delhi, wrote this poem in her honor:

FOR THREE YEARS IN WHICH HER HAND WAS STRONG
No one laid a finger on one of her orders.
In the fourth, since the page had turned from her matters.
The pen of fate drew a line through her.

. . .

Eventually, fate will draw a line through us all, emperor or commoner. But I had things to do. I had a new life to chart, other battles to fight. I had to chart a new path in life, create another type of destiny. I had drawn a line under one part of my life. It was time to begin another life altogether.

Chapter Two

चमक उठी सन सत्तावन में, वह तलवार पुरानी थी,
 The ancient sword shone like new again in 1757.
 From the mouths of bards and of minstrels of Bundelkhand we often heard this tale.
 How bravely she fought as a man-woman, the Queen of Jhansi.
 (Subhadra Kumari Chauhan, 1930)
 Rani Lakshmi Bai of Jhansi (1853-1858)

Summer of 2012, I sat in air-conditioned comfort and watched through the large, tinted windows of the train I rode in as the scrubby, sunbaked landscape rushed past. The chug of wheels flying over the rails kept time with the rhythm of my mental recitation of Subhadra Kumari Chauhan's poem. Chauhan was a female poet from my hometown, Allahabad, and the poem, one of my favorites, was about the iconic warrior queen of Jhansi, Lakshmi Bai. I repeated the only verse I remembered as the train sped toward Jhansi, a town I imagined to be almost equal in stature to its famous queen.

Roughly thirty years ago, when I was about eight years old, I rode on another train that pulled into that same station in Jhansi. I remember that trip because I had just learned Chauhan's famous poem in school and its subject—Lakshmi Bai—captured my imagination. Even the black writing on the bright yellow background that spelled out Jhansi somehow seemed magical.

Memory of that train stop in Jhansi all those years ago got me thinking about writing a book on the warrior queens of India. It was partly an engrossing project and partly a distraction from the emotionally draining pressures of a long-drawn-out adoption process my husband of sixteen years and I had initiated that year. I needed to escape the boring minutiae of that time. That's why, in the summer of 2012, I found myself on a train headed for Jhansi more than thirty years after I had first passed through the city. Jhansi is where Lakshmi Bai's story began. She was probably India's most well-known and respected female hero. She was one of the only female freedom fighters against the British, featured in my school history books and loomed large in popular culture.

The illustration of Lakshmi Bai in my school history book was a simple black-and-white sketch by an unknown artist. Lakshmi was portrayed from the waist up, hair obscured under a masculine turban, curved sword held up, face at a three-quarters angle as if captured in motion. Though inextrica

bly linked with Jhansi, the queen started her life as a little girl named Manikarnika or Manu, as she was affectionately called. While researching her early life, I discovered that she had in fact grown up in Benaras, a mere fifty-five miles away from Allahabad, my hometown. How she came to live there is woven into the strands of India's colonial history.

The young Manu grew up far from her ancestral homeland because of events that had happened centuries before she was born. In 1608, the British East India Company arrived at the court of the Mughal Emperor Jahangir to obtain his royal support to engage in trade with India. Gradually, through additional orders of patronage, the ultimate decline of the Mughal empire, and wars and annexations, the British East India Company owned India by 1763. An entire country was ruled by a corporation.

One such kingdom defeated and annexed by the Company was the powerful Maratha empire in the west. Manu's father, Moropat Tambe had been an advisor, as his forefathers had been to the Maratha rulers. When the Marathas were defeated, the king was deposed and exiled. Among those who followed the ruler was the Tambe family. The small community settled in Benaras on the banks of the holy river, Ganga. Manu was born in that ancient, holy city, between 1826 and 1832. An exact date has proven impossible to find. Even as a girl, she had a reputation of being strong and fearless. One of her childhood playmates was Nanasaheb, son of the unseated ruler of the Maratha kingdom.

I too grew up in an ancient city, the holiest site for Hindus, the city of Allahabad. It sits at the confluence of the two great Indian rivers: Ganga and Jamuna, that merge with the invisible Saraswati River. Unlike Manu, who grew up learning horseback riding, statecraft, and combat, I lived an ordinary life. I was a daydreamer, especially once I discovered the exploits of this fearless girl, who had grown up an eon ago just down the river Ganga from me.

At fourteen, I was in tenth grade. At fourteen, Manu was married to the aging, childless widower, Raja Gangadhar Rao Niwalkar, the Maratha leader of Jhansi, a far-flung vassal state located in northern India. Rumors of homosexuality, cross-dressing, and impotence dogged the king. In those hyper-masculine times, such rumors would damage any ruler's reputation. He was a physically and emotionally fragile man. Gaining a strong, young queen was politically expedient. In fact, there were suggestions that Lakshmi was chosen by his advisors and the nobility precisely because of her strength of character and courage to counterbalance the king's supposed deficiencies.

After the wedding, she assumed the name, Lakshmi, the goddess of wealth and victory, one of the milder avatars of Shakti, the source of all feminine power in the universe. Three years later, the young queen became pregnant. She was barely eighteen when she gave birth to a son, heir to the throne of Jhansi. However, three months later, the baby died. As tough as the loss of her son was for Lakshmi, the death of his long-awaited heir plunged the king into depression, and he became severely ill. He retired from public view, leaving his young queen to take on the burdens of governance. At nineteen, she became the de facto ruler of Jhansi and made all the important decisions.

Lakshmi Bai had to put aside her own grief and trauma to support her husband and Jhansi. She went on with the business of living and ruling and proved her mettle as the Queen of Jhansi. The pressures of being a wife and a ruling queen while dealing with the emotional and physical impacts of her loss are almost incomprehensible to me. Almost.

I have no child nurtured by and born of my body, which gives me some understanding of the complex feelings of being childless. Despite living in more modern times, I had internalized the belief that sustaining another human within my body and giving birth was indivisible from my womanhood. So, I always believed I was somehow deficient because the thought of having a child was anathema to me.

In 2003, when I was thirty-six, my biological clock sputtered to life.

Despite my continued ambivalence, a battle waged between my mind, which vacillated from *I should, I shouldn't*, and my body, which cried out to have a child. My brain knew the idea of having children was silly, but my heart melted at the sight of babies. I even gushed over tiny clothes. My body eventually conquered my brain and became the queen of my mind.

Underneath all this confusion, I faced a physical reality shared by tens of millions of other women; Polycystic Ovarian Syndrome (PCOS) that made pregnancy a near impossibility. My condition had been nothing than a minor annoyance—until I became obsessed with having a child.

I tried cajoling my body to conceive as if by sheer will my reluctant ovaries—studded with their many stubborn cysts—would spring to life. Despite regular visits to the fertility clinic, the many medical tests, medications, procedures, and shots I gave myself in my belly, I did not conceive.

I eventually realized that mixed with my frustration and desperation was the sinking feeling about the whole assisted reproduction process. I felt dehumanized. I imagined myself a cow and the entire process as some kind of animal husbandry. Which, in a way was accurate. I had been reduced to the sum total of my ovaries, my fallopian tubes, and my womb. I was nothing else and no one else.

I realized that I wanted a child, but not by trying to force my body into something that felt unnatural, artificial. Forcing myself just felt wrong in some way. I am no believer in destiny, but it dawned on me that becoming pregnant and giving birth was not for me.

My thoughts and emotions—and my body—rejected the process. After a few months, I had to stop. I took time off to write, pick up some freelance editorial work, be a wife to my husband, and mom to my beloved dog, Naina. My biological clock stopped as suddenly as it had started. I got used to the idea of being me again, enjoying my carefree life, playing with other people's babies, and being the fun aunt for my nieces and nephews. Time accelerated, and thirty-six became a receding memory in the rear-view mirror.

In 2005, we moved to Geneva, Switzerland for my husband's job, and childlessness became a permanent fact of life. I enjoyed the spontaneity of travel, without thinking about anything other than having a good time. The years in Switzerland flitted by like a dream.

In 2010, we returned to the United States. On January 26, 2012, I turned forty-five and out of nowhere the longing for a child roared to life again. The feeling continued to intensify over the following weeks and months. My biological clock had mutated and the desire for a child was divorced from wanting to get pregnant and give birth. Adoption, I decided, was the answer. I had never been so sure of anything in my life. It was more than sure. My decision brought a peace that the desire to get pregnant hadn't.

I researched the process, decided against going outside the country, and selected an ethical, well-regarded domestic adoption agency in Northampton, MA. Since we lived in the Boston area, having an agency just a forty-five-minute drive away appealed to us. During this time, while researching Lakshmi Bai's contribution to the Indian rebellion of 1857, I learned about her trouble bearing children and her eventual decision to adopt a son. I felt her life mirrored my modern life.

As the train slowed and entered the outskirts of Jhansi, I surveyed the uniquely Indian haphazard collection of buildings that stretched out as far as the eye could see. The train squealed to a stop, and I exited along with the crowd out into the crackling heat. I rushed to catch an air-conditioned taxi from among the cars idling alongside the station. I had booked a room in a hotel that had once been a palace in the nearby small kingdom of Orchcha a few miles from Jhansi. The rooms encircled two large, grassy courtyards and I was lucky enough to get a ground floor room with a small, stone balcony overlooking the Betwa river. I spent my first afternoon there, drinking tea, listening to music, and journaling the day's events in my trip diary.

I read over my notes, especially the information concerning the process of Lakshmi Bai's adoption, the act that would ultimately lead her to war and martyrdom. After the loss of her baby, she didn't get pregnant again. Her husband, the king, remained withdrawn from matters of state, leaving them to her. Already in ill-health, he quickly deteriorated.

In 1853, when Lakshmi Bai was around twenty-seven, a day before her husband's death, the royal couple adopted a boy from within the clan. This was a common practice and a time-honored tradition among Indian kingdoms to ensure succession and continuity. The validity of such successions had never been questioned. Things, however, were changing.

Lord Dalhousie, the British governor general for the Company, had just recently enacted a new law, the Doctrine of Lapse. This law declared that a kingdom automatically became part of the British Empire if the kingdom failed to produce an heir. Succession by adoption was deemed invalid.

When informed about the lapse of her kingdom, the newly widowed young queen is reported to have stated, *"Mein apni Jhansi nahin doongee."* I will never give up my Jhansi.

Jhansi was hers to safeguard until she could hand the kingdom over to her son. However, Lakshmi Bai was no match for the British and, in 1854, she was forced to retire with her son and their attendants to a small house in the city. She lived there for almost four years on an annual pension of sixty thousand rupees. However, she didn't give up hope. Things were changing. Rumors reached her that something big was about to happen. She might be able to secure the kingdom for Damodar Rao, after all.

The fort of Jhansi sits on a rugged, rocky hill, easily visible from almost every vantage point in the new, larger, modern city. Before the current massive urban expansion, the fort must have provided a three-hundred-and-sixty-degree view of the open landscape, enabling its inhabitants to be aware of an enemy's approach.

My taxi wheezed up the snaking road, tires sticking to the tarmac from the heat. The driver shut off the air-conditioning to divert power to the engine and the car became an instant sauna. Vehicles are only allowed half-way up the hill. Like all other visitors, I too had to walk the rest of the brick-lined incline up to the fort.

The driver stopped at the entrance of the fort complex. I thanked him, grabbed my ever-present bottle of water, and got out of the car. The hot, strong wind offered instant relief from the still, hot air inside the car. I began my slow walk up to the fort, ignoring the lazy but loud sales pitches of the water and tea sellers who had escaped the summer heat beneath broad-leafed trees. My evident lack of interest was enough incentive for them to not emerge from their shaded refuge.

At the gate, I bought my ticket from a drowsy man half-asleep on a rickety, wooden chair inside the glass-fronted booth. I also engaged the services of a local guide. I found him entertaining, despite him being less a historian than a source of Lakshmi Bai mythology and his own opinions. We stepped through the imposing main gate into a courtyard that led to the interior entrance of the compound. The sun beat down with relentless heat that fairly made the dry air crackle around us. I had consumed most of my water. Sweat stung my eyes. My guide merely wrapped his dingy checked, white and red cloth *angocha* around his head, neck, and face like a desert Bedouin.

We entered the first courtyard and there stood Lakshmi Bai's famous cannon *Kadak Bijli* (powerful lightning), mounted on a concrete platform. I had never considered that a weapon of war might be beautiful but there was no other way to describe the cannon. The dark, heavy metal glistened in the sunlight. The hazy, heated air made its solid lines appear to undulate, as if alive. Graceful vines, twining leaves and curlicues were carved in relief down its length and encircled the nozzle. I touched the metal and yanked my hand back at the burn to my fingertips. Standing in the cradle of Indian revolutionary history, I could almost hear the cannon's fiery roar in the heat of battle against the encroaching British army.

Like all Indian forts, Jhansi was constructed of stone and mortar, built to withstand battle. It was much smaller than many others and more utilitarian than beautiful. Yet the fort had stood for hundreds of years, as if the stone had sprung from the dusty soil in which it was rooted. It was a pragmatic, unadorned structure whose primary purpose was to protect those within from outside onslaughts.

The lack of any other visitors allowed me to wander silently without distraction, lost in the historical wonder of the place I had so long imagined. The guide and I came back together on the ramparts. The walls were at least a foot wider than my height of five feet three inches. The whisper of a hot breeze blew bone-dry dust past my sunglasses and into my eyes. Still, I couldn't tear my gaze from the city. On this blistering hot day, the closely clustered houses shimmered like a mirage that seemed to go on forever.

The centuries-old stones beneath my sandals had been contemporary to Lakshmi Bai. Repairs had been done to damaged sections of the wall, scars from long-ago battles. Perhaps Rani Lakshmi Bai had stood exactly where I now stood and watched as the British lay siege to the city on March 22, 1858. Though she was safe inside the walls of the fort, she had no choice but to mount a futile defense of her city and its citizens.

I asked the guide if any of the old city remained after the violent rampage on April 2, 1858, and he said no. By some accounts, before that dark day in April, Lakshmi Bai had explored all options, including relinquishing Jhansi to the Company and raising her son in a mansion in the city. Damodar Rao, her child, had become the focus of her life and keeping him alive and safe remained her chief concern.

By 1857, mutinies against the Company had broken out all across India, which then became a larger revolution. The rebels needed a figurehead, a nominal leader to fight for, so they rallied around the aging and frail Mughal emperor who ruled in name only. Emperor Bahadur Shah Zafar went from presiding over an impoverished, empty court to becoming the leader of this new revolution. But the powerful Mughal army of yore was gone and Emperor Bahadur Shah Zafar was too old to lead a rebellion. The real leaders of the revolution were Lakshmi Bai's childhood friend Nanasaheb and his general, Tantya Tope. Clearly, the revolution filled Lakshmi Bai with hope, and she threw in her lot with the rebellion. Perhaps this was her final hope to take back her kingdom and safeguard it for Damodar Rao.

She retook the fort and threw out the small contingent

posted there. Lakshmi Bai was again the ruler of Jhansi, living in her official residence. The walls of the fort had been fortified. She supervised the training of her army, which now included new volunteers, the most well-known fighting force composed of Jhansi women who vowed to defend the kingdom. Lakshmi Bai also negotiated with friendly neighboring kingdoms to provide reinforcements for when the British army finally attacked in 1858.

The city walls fell to British cannons and soldiers poured in and bayoneted any resident within reach of their blades. As homes were looted and vandalized and the city was virtually destroyed, Lakshmi Bai anxiously awaited the arrival of the huge, twenty thousand strong Maratha army led by her childhood friend Nanasaheb.

The much hoped for reinforcements never arrived.

Later, she would learn why. The Maratha army had camped nearby in Kalpi. This proved to be a major miscalculation, for while they were encamped, the much smaller British army merely marched around them to Jhansi. The Marathas lost this battle. The British, on the other hand, made every effort to capture the queen with the intent to humiliate and make an example of her.

There is nothing in my life that can compare to the life of this iconic queen. But I can identify with her in one singular way. I—like many mothers—would do anything to safeguard my child. Lakshmi Bai faced the challenges of a queen and was willing to go to war to protect her child. As much as I abhor violence and war, if I had to fight to keep my child safe, I would chuck my pacifism and fight.

I felt Lakshmi Bai's same unshakable certainty barely six months later in January 2013, as I held my daughter in an anonymous hotel room in the middle of America. Her eyes were closed but the moment the nipple of the bottle touched her mouth she opened wide and latched on as if she knew this whole life business was all about survival above all else. I smoothed her silky eyebrows, the delicate skin of her cheeks, and knew that I was ready to kill and to be killed to protect this tiny person.

Rani Lakshmi Bai remained undaunted by the defeat and lack of reinforcements and continued to fight. She was determined to fight alongside her troops to the death, but an old tribal chief exhorted the queen to escape to fight another day, for dying by one of the British bullets would be *"as useless as dying an ignoble a death."*

Only when all seemed lost did she at last agree to flee her ravaged city and retreat behind the still intact walls of her fort. Then she plotted an escape for Damodar Rao and herself. When it came down to his life or his right to rule, Lakshmi Bai chose his life. Any mother would do the same.

The British General Hugh Rose anticipated her escape and withdrew his guards from the north facing Bhanderi Gate of the fort in preparation of an ambush. Lakshmi Bai knew about the trap. She had no option but to fight, but wouldn't have left secretly, even if she could have. Lakshmi Bai would not show fear. Accompanied by her retinue of trusted Afghan guards, and carrying her son on her back, she rode through the city to bid a sad farewell to her people. She carried no money, nothing valuable, except her silver drinking cup and the ornaments she wore beneath her masculine clothing. Despite her public departure, perhaps helped by the noisy chaos of the plundered city, she made it outside the ruined city walls with her pursuers hard on her heels.

A furious gun-battle ensued as she got out of the city. D.V. Tahmankar's book, *The Ranee of Jhansi*, details the escape. The British soldiers reported her perfect riding skills. Astride her horse Chetak, reins clenched between her teeth, she gripped a sword in each hand. Fighting fiercely, she managed to escape her pursuers and, in doing so, humiliated General Rose. Capturing or killing the Queen of Jhansi became the general's personal quest and he sent his own lieutenant after her.

The lieutenant charged with capturing her related his story to Colonel R. G. Button, *"I was gaining fast on the Ranee, who with four attendants was escaping on a grey horse, when I was dismounted by a severe wound and would have been almost cut in half but that the blow was turned by the revolver on my hip. I was thus obliged to give up the pursuit and the lady escaped for the time being."*

Jhansi is in the Bundelkhand region of Madhya Pradesh. I had traversed this hard baked, furrowed, and rocky earth with its treacherous ravines by train. Despite the inhospitable and forbidding terrain, there is a certain wild beauty to the land. A faint haze of talcum-powder fine dust is ever-present.

Lakshmi Bai rode nonstop and covered the one hundred and two miles of rough terrain to Kalpi in roughly twenty-four hours. Despite the many skirmishes along the way, she arrived safely with her son.

I thought about her frantic journey when, months later, I made my own twenty-four-hour mad dash across continents to be with my daughter. From the moment my phone rang in that darkened train car in India with news of my daughter's birth in America, life accelerated at super-sonic speed. The most trying part was having to sit still, impatiently watching time pass as the train grew increasingly more delayed. Eventually I arrived in my hometown of Allahabad at two p.m. just three hours before the ancient, propeller plane on which I had booked my flight was to depart. I lunched with my mother at our favorite restaurant *El Chico*, then rushed to the tiny airport that was notorious for its frequent flight cancellations and delays.

"Please be on time. Please take off," I repeated in silent refrain, willing the plane to get me to Delhi in time for my international flight back to the States. I willed myself not to think about the stories of flights cancelled with the passengers already boarded or while taxiing because of light fog or some other flimsy excuse.

As it turned out, that small plane was the only plane on time the entire journey. I arrived in Delhi at seven p.m. and hung out with my sister at her house since, like most international flights, mine departed in the early morning hours.

My sister took one look at my shell-shocked face and did her best to reassure me.

"It's really not that hard. When kids are infants all you have to do is feed them, change their diapers and keep them safe. You'll get the hang of it. You'll manage. You'll be fine."

Still, my blood ran cold, and fear of failure dominated my thoughts. Not love, not joy, but a mix of shock and impatience. Not a gush of love. Fear of failure. Fear of the magnitude of this new responsibility. Everyone was intrigued. My brother-in-law wished me well. My nephew who, despite usually being a brash teen, declared that my husband and I would be great parents. This was the first adoption for which anyone in my family had a front row seat. Even my sister's Nepali cook Ujwala was intrigued and insisted on seeing the baby's picture several times.

"Oh, she looks almost Nepali," she finally exclaimed. "And so do you. See nothing to be afraid of...she even looks like you."

I laughed because the vaguely Mongolian features that had always set me uncomfortably apart while growing up in India now seemed to be an asset instead of a liability. Perhaps my "almost Nepali" features was fate telling me that this unknown child I had claimed as daughter was meant to be mine.

Time rushed by and I departed for the Indira Gandhi International Airport. I have no memory of passport control, checking in, or even of boarding the flight, which was already three hours late. I do remember sitting cross-legged on my seat, watching movies I don't remember and barely eating because nervousness and anticipation crept back into me. I tried snuggling up in a blanket to sleep but remained wide-awake throughout the eighteen-hour long flight to Newark.

Since the plane was over three hours late, the landing procedures had to be condensed. Predictably, after immigration and customs, and despite the mad rush to the United domestic terminal, I missed my flight to Chicago O'Hare—which was a connecting flight to Indiana. The check-in agents looked bored as they informed me the next flight to Chicago departed the following morning. The two women continued gossiping about another coworker, oblivious to my stress.

"You've got to help me," I blurted, "My husband is waiting for me in Chicago. We're adopting a little girl. She arrived early and I've been awake for twenty-four hours...and I need to get there." The words tumbled out of me.

They stared. I whipped out my phone and pulled up the baby pictures my husband had sent me. They visibly melted and called over agents from other airline counters to coo over the pictures.

One of them finally said, "Okay, let's see what we can do."

She bent the rules and booked me on a Delta flight even though I didn't fulfill the requirements for being rebooked on another airline. She spoke with the Delta agent a few desks over and confirmed me for the eight p.m. flight to Chicago. I thanked them profusely, then rushed toward the gate, their good wishes ringing in my ears. I had successfully—for the first time—used the magic of a new baby.

I reached O'Hare and raced through its long walkways and high-ceilinged terminal. They held the plane to Indianapolis long enough for me to board. I was almost there, where I needed to be. Excitement and terror swirled in my stomach.

I stumbled off the plane in Indianapolis at nearly midnight. Then I saw my husband in Arrivals. His expression mirrored my exhaustion and tension, but I easily read the glaze of new love in his eyes. I remember the hour-long drive to our final destination, the wide Indiana highways, and the few vehicles on the roads because it was past midnight. I didn't realize I'd dozed off until I awoke to find we had arrived at the hospital.

I couldn't turn back now. Taking a deep, shaky breath, I squared my shoulders and walked with my husband through the main entrance. The security guard recognized my husband and waved us through to the elevator for the maternity floor. A nurse ushered us into the "new mommy room" where my husband had spent the last thirty-six hours. I washed and sanitized every part of my exposed skin, then draped myself in a sterile hospital-issue sheet and sat in the easy chair by the bed.

My crazy journey across continents and through the United States had brought me to my goal, to finally hold my infant daughter in my arms. It was a satisfying end to a journey and the start of a calmer life. Rani Lakshmi Bai's twenty-four-hour hard ride, however, was not the end of her journey, but merely the beginning of even harder times.

She arrived at Kalpi exhausted and devastated by the destruction of her city. Various accounts detail her meeting with Nanasaheb, once her childhood friend, now the Peshwa in exile, the king of the Marathas. As she walked toward Peshwa Nanasaheb, she was both queen of the Maratha vassal state of Jhansi and a loyal—though disgruntled—subject. Within the constraints of leader-subordinate etiquette, how could she convey her displeasure about the shoddy war strategy that had cost her Jhansi and the lives of so many of her people?

After the barest of polite greetings, she laid her unsheathed sword, the symbol of her realm's fealty to the Marathas, in front of the Peshwa. She confronted him with her characteristic forthrightness, saying, *"Your Highness's illustrious forbears presented this weapon to us and with its powerful help we used it to do what was just and proper. But now that we cannot have your support I beg to return it to you."* (Tahmankar, 1958).

The discomfited and embarrassed Peshwa praised her valiant defense of Jhansi and for having the courage and foresight to leave when she did, which to him proved her, "military skill and courage." He also said, *"I beg you to take back this sword and give me all your support in my struggle."* It was a struggle he called *"our ideal of independence."*

She relented, assured of his ongoing support, accepted his regrets, and reasserted her loyalty. I imagine she had few choices. I also imagine her, exhausted and aching, gutted by the nightmarish memories of her city's destruction. It was inevitable that she would agree to join forces with Nanasaheb. He also understood that she had needed to express her despair and anger at being abandoned during her hour of need. Perhaps she too needed something to believe in. Anything.

"Nothing," she said, *"will give me greater happiness than to die on the battlefield, serving the Mahratta standard."*

What drove her? Allegiance to the Marathas? A desire to

reign over Jhansi, again? To keep Jhansi secure and strong before handing the city over to her son? Or had her motivation evolved to encompass the idea of a pan-Indian independence that had been gaining momentum since the revolution began in 1857?

There is no doubt that her paramount motivation was to protect Damodar Rao. She trusted no one—not even her loyal Afghan bodyguards—to keep him safe. Instead, she kept him close. Even during the long and harsh ride to Kalpi, he remained tied to her back with a silken sheet. More than just safeguarding his future throne, she kept him alive and safe with a maternal ferocity similar to India's powerful mother goddesses, Durga and Kali.

When the nurse wheeled the baby's crib into the room where my husband and I waited, terror trickled through my veins. She was so tiny. Would I manage? Oh my god, what was I supposed to do if she started choking? Babies choke when being fed, right? What if I dropped her? She was so fragile, this little life that had been entrusted to my care. There was no time to react before the nurse nestled the sleeping bundle in my sheet-draped arms. She weighed a scant six pounds but the weight of the massive responsibility of her care seemed to almost crush me.

I closed my eyes. When I opened them, again, she was staring straight at me. Her mouth rounded into an O as she yawned widely. I touched a finger to her forehead where the delicate skin was flaking off white. One of her little arms had come loose from her swaddle and she grabbed my finger and held tight. Just like that, we connected.

"Hi," I whispered, "Hi, baby."

Her intense newborn stare remained on my face. I took the bottle of formula the nurse offered and brushed the nipple against her mouth. She immediately latched on and started feeding, eyes now half-closed in ecstasy. She was a fighter, this one. She had already endured a monumental separation from her birth mother, a trauma in the first hours of her life. She knew there was no time to lose fussing over the little things. No time or energy for any feeding issues or anything else.

As she drank still holding my finger, a thought occurred to me. I was holding the hand of the person who would probably hold my hand at the end of my life. And so the cycle of life continues. I smiled at her as if we had shaken on some pact. She snuffled softly, eyes almost fully closed now, tummy full. I hugged her closer, content in her warmth and the steady up and down rhythm of her chest.

I imagined I felt as Lakshmi Bai probably felt when Damodar Rao became her son. He was her responsibility, yes. But he was also her inspiration, her motivation, her mission, her love. She was ready to die or kill for him, to do whatever she had to keep him safe.

The day I entered the darkened, echoing near-emptiness of the Jhansi Museum, we experienced a power outage—as was common in Jhansi and most other small town in India. An eerie silence hung in the air. No whirring of the ceiling fan, buzzing of the tube-lights, all the sounds that come along with electricity. Sweat covered my face, gluing my hair to my forehead. Not a breath of air moved in the building, though the sun still shone pitilessly through the wide-open windows.

I stopped in front of a painting of the warrior queen and peered at it through dust-coated glass. Rani Lakshmi Bai sits in a chair, with a British soldier, red-coated and erect seated in another right beside her. She wore white, the color of widows, but was adorned with gold anklets and ornate green shoes to display her royal status. In her right hand she held her curved sword. The is soldier is staring at the floor, while Lakshmi Bai looks directly into the camera.

Painted by an unknown folk artist, the picture is whimsical, off-scale, and totally unrealistic. Still, the picture managed to accurately illustrate how the people of Bundelkhand saw their most iconic heroine. Pure, chaste, brave, and fierce. Even sitting beside the symbol of her colonial oppressor, she is calm and unafraid.

She has been described by some British historians as beautiful, and merely ordinary by others. I am unable to discern, to judge whether she is what might be considered beautiful. Her expression is serene, unflinching, stoic, and determined. I discern no sense that she is intimidated by the embodiment of colonial power seated next to her. I look into her large, wide painted eyes and she and I are alone in that empty, dusty, quiet room.

Clicking sounds jarred me from the trance and the lights blazed to life and rainbows reflected from the glass cases across the walls. A group of loud people entered the portrait hall and I walked out back into the unrelenting sun where a breeze dried the sweat on my face.

Early the next morning, I took the train to Gwalior, the city that was Lakshmi Bai's next destination with the rebel army. The landscape flying past looked as if it had jumped out of a legend: hazy, indistinct, stained by the distance and the weight of history. I easily imagined the Maratha army marching past, led by Lakshmi Bai, Nanasaheb, and Tantya Tope.

The princely state of Gwalior was a vassal of the British, loyal to the Company. Some nobles and most of the rank and file of the Gwalior army wanted to join the rebellion. However, the powerful Prime Minister Dinkar Rao maintained the small kingdom's loyalty to the British. He was the real power in the kingdom, as the young king Jayaji Rao Scindia was heavily influenced by him.

Eventually, the rebel forces reached Gwalior, and the leaders met with King Jayaji Rao Scindia and Prime Minister Dinkar Rao in a vain attempt to convince them to join their cause. Upon their steadfast refusal, the rebel army attacked, and easily captured, the fort. This quick victory was largely due to the enthusiastic support of Gwalior's army that had joined them. Dinkar Rao and Jayaji Rao managed to escape. The victorious army took down the flag of Gwalior and flew the rebel flag from its flagpole.

After having been defeated in various skirmishes along the way, the rebel army found a solid base in Gwalior. Despite their victory over Gwalior, they were exhausted, strained for resources, and fast losing their fervor for freedom. News filtered in of the resurgent and much larger and well-equipped British army that was winning more battles than it was losing. The corpses of rebels and their sympathizers hung from trees across the country and entire villages were razed to the ground.

Added to that, Nanasaheb and Tope, until now carried along by the rebellion's momentum and the loyalty of their troops, began making critical errors. Exhausted and feeling secure behind the walls of the fort, they let down their guard. Only Lakshmi Bai remained on high alert. She knew something big was going to happen. She also knew they couldn't stay in Gwalior forever. Gwalior was merely a reprieve not a destination.

With the lull in action, schisms began to appear between the leaders. Despite Lakshmi Bai's prowess and military strategy, the bulk of the army followed Tantya Tope who was known as an experienced general. Lakshmi Bai was a relatively new warrior, and a woman at that. This decision would cost them and the independence movement dearly.

In Gwalior, I stayed at the luxurious heritage hotel, the Taj Usha Kiran Palace, once owned by the ruling family the Scindias. Built in 1880, this five-star palace turned hotel epitomizes luxury, from the opulent and discreetly modernized suites to the beautiful ornately carved stone walls. Each time I walked its wide, cool, serpentine corridors, I felt as if I had stepped back in time. As lovely as my stay was, however, I'd chosen the hotel not because of its proximity to the sites I needed to visit in Gwalior, but because it was near the Jai Vilas Palace, the main residence of the Scindias, which was now a museum.

The palace was constructed after Lakshmi Bai was in Gwalior around 1874. The Scindias were British collaborators and, Jai Vilas, their primary palace, showcased the lavish rewards this allegiance bestowed upon them. The building is strangely fantastical and over the top with a fully functional, miniature silver train that runs along tiny tracks set in the long dining table. The silver train would carry after-dinner brandy and cigars for royal guests and stopped when one of the crystal decanters was lifted from the train. Massive chandeliers of various colors hung in the ostentatiously decorated rooms that made the royal residence in Jhansi seem almost destitute in comparison—especially when you add the bubbling fountains found in many of the guest rooms.

I found Jai Vilas Palace strange and over-done, but I was there to see a rather humble artifact, a tangible item that once belonged to Rani Lakshmi Bai: her shield. This was the closest I would come to her physical presence. I wandered through the museum that also included armors from the Mughal kings and a tapestry that depicted the rulers of Europe and India.

Then I saw what I'd come for.

A large round knob that bears the face of the sun is set in the middle of the shield. Four smaller knobs are located at four "corners" about halfway on the shield's dull-black surface. The *dhal* was no showpiece. A myriad of scratches, slices, and gouges mark this dhal as a well-used weapon. I envisioned the swords, lances, and daggers Lakshmi Bai must have repelled in battle. How wrong that this personal piece of her property should be in the opulent palace of her enemy.

The next day, I hired a guide and headed farther away from the hotel to the Gwalior fort. The opulence of the building clearly said that this too had been the stronghold of a rich kingdom. Though its defenses were strong and its walls and fortifications solid and impenetrable this was no mere utilitarian fort as was Jhansi. Inlays or elaborate carvings adorned many of the buildings. As we passed through the main gates into a large courtyard, a middle-aged woman with salt and pepper hair headed straight toward me.

"You are taking pictures? Lakshmi Bai, huh?" she asked.

The guide shooed her away, calling her crazy, and muttering about how he was sick of her harassing tourists. I spoke to her, however, as the guide fumed and continued to mutter about tourists encouraging these pests who always wanted money.

"Yes, I am taking pictures," I told her. "How did you know what I am here for?"

"I just know." She smiled. "Come,"—she squared her shoulders—"take a photograph of me."

I framed her in my shot and clicked. As I got ready to hand her some money, she turned and walked away without a word.

As I write this, I stare at her photograph taped to my computer. Her hair is uncombed, rough with dust and sun, her sari the color of mud. Incongruously, instead of a blouse, she wears a tan corduroy jacket with a shearling collar over the sari, despite the heat. She looks straight at me, her gaze unafraid, inscrutable.

I know that out of frame, but beside her, is the beautifully ornate Maan Singh Palace, decorated with intricate patterns of blue and yellow tiles, now crumbling but still brilliant. The stone bears scars from the British assault. One of its towers is shorter than the others, decapitated by British cannonballs.

Though the rebel leaders, Lakshmi Bai, Nanasaheb, and Tantya Tope, were now the de-facto rulers of Gwalior, the reprieve was temporary. While Lakshmi Bai knew the British would attack, General Tantya Tope and Nanasaheb weren't quite so sure.

Tope and Nanasaheb repeatedly ignored her advice and warnings. Did they do so because she was a woman and war was a man's game? There are no records of them alluding to her gender in their short-sighted decisions, but ingrained habits die hard, and misogyny was the norm.

There are reports that she was disappointed by the lack of military vigor among Tope's troops. The Maratha troops, exhausted from their months-long campaigns and thrilled by their victory, spent their time raiding the royal treasury, drinking and taking it easy. Their battle-readiness degraded by the day. Frustrated, Lakshmi Bai took over their training, but it was a doomed cause. While Jhansi's soldiers and some others followed her lead, most did not. Meanwhile, the British rallied, and they had a well-disciplined and well-funded army. In contrast, the rebel armies were fragmented, led by generals of varying levels of experience and ability. One-by-one, the superior British forces crushed rebel strongholds, capturing or killing the leaders, razing entire villages and towns. They left behind blackened, smoking ruins and thousands of bodies swinging from trees.

This juggernaut marched toward Gwalior and there was no escape. The rebels realized that they were isolated and alone, their allies routed and destroyed. The British lay siege to the fort with a severe and unrelenting bombardment. As Lakshmi Bai feared, the Maratha troops were ill-prepared and confused. The cannons boomed and eventually breached the walls of the fort. All was lost.

Like most people, I've been lucky to never have experienced war. However, like most other people and like Lakshmi Bai, I have been in a place where all available options lead only to undesirable conclusions. For me, that moment arrived when we first considered adoption. In 2008, we lived in Switzerland, had endured an invasive home-study, and decided to adopt from India in hopes of ensuring the child's cultural integration was less challenging.

India had tightened restrictions on international adoptions with the objective of placing adoptees with families within the country. Add to that India's layers of red tape and its infamous delays, we might have been matched with a child at birth only to be forced to wait for years before being able to bring him or her home. I know of a couple who finally got their child when he was seven. There was also growing concern about human trafficking. The government discovered that some adoptees were kidnapping victims, which lead to even more stringent requirements for adoptive parents.

While at an appointment with our Swiss adoption agency, my husband and I looked at each other, confident we could side-step any complications of the Indian system. We were also pleased because we expected the process to be much faster than it would have been in the U.S.. Switzerland had a tiny population of just six million. How many potential adoptive families could there possibly be?

"We're Indian," we informed the agency representative meeting us.

"But you are U.S. Citizens, no?" the representative asked.

That's when we learned that as far as India was concerned, the fact we were Indian made no difference. For the purposes of adoption, we fell into the same category as any foreigner from any country. There were no exceptions. Once we renounced Indian citizenship, our Indianness was no longer recognized by the country of our birth. Wait times for an international adoption was five to seven years. Adopting a Swiss child wasn't an option because we weren't citizens and, in any case, they preferred placing adoptees with those who shared their culture and heritage. We came to a screeching halt, unsure how to proceed. No matter how I tried to think my way around this obstacle, I saw no solution. A family friend visiting us from India had a novel solution.

He advised me to consider living in India for a year or two while my husband visited regularly. He would plug us into a network of OB/GYNs who often had patients wanting to give up their babies secretly and without scandal. One of these babies would be mine, and a few months later I'd return home acting out a charade that I got pregnant and gave birth in India.

Apart from the obvious ethical challenges, if things went wrong, we risked being accused and convicted of human trafficking and fraud. I wanted a child, but I had no intention of preying on a desperate birth mother with few real choices, nor did I want to go to prison. I could see no path forward and our adoption efforts dissolved into nothingness.

Like a depressing chess game, no matter the move I

contemplated, I lost. In a way, I felt a sense of relief. If anyone asked, the decision was out of my hands. I wanted to have a child, but from infertility to the impossibility of adoption, the universe had conspired against me. We had reached an impasse and I still firmly believed that not having a child wasn't the end of the world. When all avenues are closed off, one must accept the inevitable with as much grace as one can muster.

After our adoption plans fizzled, I threw myself into writing, travel, spending time with friends and family, and my job as an acquisitions and development editor for a German American company. Then I was laid off and I realized how much of my self-esteem and purpose was tied to that job. In an inevitable pattern, I headed straight down the path to depression. I steadied myself with medication and lots and lots of exercise. I filled my hours with activities and a social life I never had before or since. Time marched in place while my age accelerated at an alarming rate.

In the summer of 2010, while out looking at a house we were considering moving to in Geneva, I got a call from my husband. I thought he had called to find out more about the house. We were both excited about the large, rambling, quirky home with brightly colored, carved wooden bannisters and pillars. But he hadn't called about the house. After five years in beautiful Geneva, we were headed back to the U.S. By November of that same year, we had moved back to Massachusetts.

Life lurched into a new trajectory and suddenly we had options. We weren't sure where these options would lead us, but they existed. Just as new options presented themselves for the Queen of Jhansi when all other options had been considered and discarded. Luckily for me, my new situation led me to a much happier direction than did hers. History remembers her for the choice she made. I have no desire for a place in history.

With the enemy at the gates, like the warrior she was, Lakshmi Bai accepted the inevitable and knew this would be her final battle. She and the other rebel leaders knew that being captured by the British would be a humiliating defeat. The "Indian Jezebel," was the most well-known rebel leader. General Rose had a personal vendetta against her. She would be made an example of and that was something her pride would not allow. Still, she refused to slink away like a coward.

Rani Lakshmi Bai and her escorts—two female warriors dressed as men and some of her Afghan guards—readied themselves for their final battle. At the appointed time, amid the chaos of battle, they flung open the huge iron-studded, wooden main gates of Gwalior fort.

The queen and her coterie thundered out on horseback and broke through the cordon of British soldiers. For once, Damodar Rao was not with his mother. She had commended him to her most trusted guard Ram Chandra Rao, who snuck out through a smaller side gate during of the commotion of the resulting confusion. Lakshmi Bai and her warriors fought their way through the British defenses and escaped. Pursuit was inevitable and the Hussars, a military unit modeled on the Hungarian light cavalry, gained on the escapees. It is unclear if the pursuers realized exactly who they were chasing, just that they were after some escaping rebels.

As Lakshmi Bai and her warriors galloped through the surrounding countryside, one of her female guards was shot. The queen wheeled around to fight and successfully killed some of their pursuers. Then they fled. However, her horse had been injured and balked at jumping over a ditch. The delay allowed their pursuers to catch up to them and they were quickly surrounded.

Many of us have experienced that sensation of being closed in, when everything telescopes into two tight choices: surrender or fight. Luckily, most have never faced a life or death choice. I wonder what she felt when she gripped her two swords and hacked her way through an enemy that was sure to triumph over her.

The queen and her guards were hopelessly outnumbered. Most of her men and the remaining female guard were killed. One of the Hussars shot her. Another slashed at her head with his sword and sliced off her eye. When she fell to the ground, a third soldier bayoneted her. The soldiers had no idea they had mortally wounded the iconic warrior queen but assumed they had killed a male warrior of the rank and file. They left her where she lay and continued their pursuit of the other rebels who had escaped.

Miraculously, though covered with blood and close to death, she was still alive when her devoted servant Ram Chandra Rao arrived. The seven-year-old Prince Damodar Rao sat behind him on the horse. Rao carried his queen to the nearby hut of sage Ganga Das. There she drank some water, including holy water from the Ganga as part of her last rites. The queen was lucid enough to give funeral instructions to Ram Chandra Rao. Then she looked at Damodar one last time and died. Years later, Damodar Rao would talk about that moment for it was a memory that never left him.

Following her instructions to make sure her body didn't fall into British hands, Ram Chandra Rao cremated her remains and burned the sage's hut in which she lay. Once satisfied that no trace of her body remained, he left with Damodar Rao. The date was June 18, 1858.

The warrior queen who had gone to war to protect her son and his rights was unsuccessful in her quest to secure the kingdom. She did leave him with a legacy of heroism and an agreement she had negotiated with the British that left him well provided for. The compromise she had come to—before joining the rebellion—was that even though Damodar could not become the ruler of Jhansi, he could inherit his father's personal wealth. This was not to be, however.

The hotel suite where my husband and I sequestered with our new baby, sat off a busy state highway. Fast food joints and chain restaurants of every kind lined each side of the road and were interspersed with mega-stores and strip malls. We waited in suspended animation for judges from our home state and the state the baby was born in to give us permission to return home. This process can take anywhere from a week to a month, sometimes more, was the unhelpful response to our queries. While we existed in limbo, our hotel suite filled up with all the supplies every tiny baby needs, from microwaveable sanitizer to a bassinet, bottles, formula, tons of diapers, and tiny clothes. Each day of the delay, we accumulated even more.

Our focus remained on feeding, changing, and cuddling our newborn. In retrospect, I realize how lucky we were to have this time of introspection and bonding with our baby with no distractions of home or work.

On January 21, 2013, we watched Barack Obama's second inauguration on TV. I can still see the scene like a snapshot, my husband stood to one side of the television. He cradled the baby in the crook of his arm and rocked her while whispering to her about the momentous occasion. She slept through the inauguration, thoroughly unimpressed.

Yet something niggled at me. Despite the fact that all my protective and caring instincts were on over-drive, I didn't feel like a mother. I felt as if I was merely playing at being one. What did being a mother feel like? Surely, being a mother was something beyond this love and concern I felt for the baby? I wasn't sure. What if I never felt like a mother, her mother? I wondered how Lakshmi Bai had felt. She gave birth to and nurtured a baby who died. Did she feel—really feel—like Damodar's mother?

Finally, the judges from both states gave us permission to take our baby home. The doctors, however, didn't clear her for flying in winter. So, we rented a van large enough to carry us and all the baby stuff that filled our hotel suite and headed home. We stopped every two hours to feed and change the baby, and to eat and use the restroom. Half-way through the seventeen-hour journey in Pennsylvania, we stopped for the night.

I don't remember the name of the off-the-highway motel. The room was anonymous as all such rooms seem to be. It was, however, freezing cold. I turned up the heat but fifteen minutes later, I was still shivering, and every surface and the sterile white bathroom were icy. I called the front to complain and was assured that the heating was slow, but it would be on.

At two a.m., the room was still as cold as when we arrived. Exhausted by the drive, my husband fell asleep wrapped in the hotel comforter and his warmest clothes. As I fed the baby, I wondered how one could tell if a baby had hypothermia...before it was too late, anyway. I was responsible for this tiny person. I had her wrapped in three blankets, but how could I be certain she was warm enough? My paranoia grew into nightmarish visions of waking up in the morning to find her frozen solid. It was clear by now that there was no heat in the room. The sullen front-desk clerk whom I had called at least half a dozen times, finally informed me that the heating system in the hotel had broken down. There was no hope of a repairman coming until the next day We were exhausted, and it was already three a.m., so we had to survive in the sub-zero temperature. It was as cold inside as out.

I hate winter clothes, but I put on my warmest sweater and the thick winter jacket I had bought from a store near the hotel. My feet are always cold, so I wore two pairs of socks. Then I nestled the baby against my chest. She nuzzled closer, milk-drunk from her last feed, and her eyes drifted shut. I sat upright against the headboard and fought sleep. I had no book and I had set my phone to charge in the only functional power outlet, at the other end of the room, but the battery died.

I kept track of the baby's fluttering regular breaths under my chin and, as so often happened, my thoughts wandered to Lakshmi Bai. With my baby warm and safe against me, I felt I could save her from anything, so long as I kept her close. It didn't escape me that Lakshmi Bai too always held her son close and must have felt as I did. Every statue and picture of Lakshmi Bai depicted her on horseback with Damodar swaddled to her back with silken cloths.

Did she also feel like I did, that she could only be assured of his safety if he remained close? As I held my baby through the night, I knew I would both die and kill for her. In that chilled quiet motel room off a now-forgotten highway, I finally felt like a mother. I tightened my arms around her and stared down into her sleeping face.

"Hey baby," I said, "I am your mother."

I didn't feel like a clueless fraud. I felt like a mother. I was a mother. Her mother. The love I had always felt for her swelled inside me but with something more, something all at once tender yet fierce, brave yet terrified. My daughter smiled in her sleep. It wasn't gas. I refuse to believe that.

"Yeah, don't you ever forget I'm your mother," I whispered.

She continued sleeping, her breathing soft and regular.

After Lakshmi Bai's death, Ram Chandra Rao and others loyal to their martyred queen, hid Damodar Rao in the rural areas around Gwalior for three days. Only sixty of Lakshmi Bai's loyal soldiers survived the war and their mission now was to ensure the safety of the orphaned prince. For months, they traveled in the tangled bush and lived in forests with little food, afraid to venture into any village or town for fear of running into soldiers in search of the prince.

Then Damodar Rao fell ill. He became increasingly frail, and his protectors feared for his life. Taking a calculated risk, in September 1858, one of them went into town and appealed to a local sympathetic British officer. In lieu of his mother, Damodar Rao surrendered and was allowed an annual pension of Rs. 10,000. However, he never received the Rs. 700,000 inheritance from his father, held in trust for him. According to the British, his father had not really been his father. According to the new law, he had no legal standing as his deceased father's heir.

He eventually settled in Indore, married, had children, and lived an ordinary life. There are verbal accounts of Damodar Rao visiting the fort when he was older, so that he could relive the memories of life with his mother. He assumed a new family name, Jhansiwale—of Jhansi—to hold fast to his heritage. No one could take that away from him.

Damodar died in May 1906 at the age of fifty-eight. His mother, Masaheb, as he respectfully called her—couldn't give him his kingdom or his wealth, but she kept him alive at the expense of her own life. She also left him with an understanding of his importance to her, an example of fierce maternal love, courage, the warrior code, and heroism. His natural parents remain obscured in history, for he will be forever known as Rani Lakshmi Bai's son.

In the months that followed Lakshmi Bai's death, Nanasaheb, Tantya Tope, and other rebel leaders were hounded, captured, and executed. Villages and towns known to have supported the rebels were erased from existence, those citizens either executed or rendered homeless. In my own hometown Allahabad, our prized posh and planned shopping center the Civil Lines was created on the site of such a carnage. Late in 1858, during one single night, eight villages were razed.

The India Company did not hold on to India for long. The British Crown was embarrassed by the chaos of the Indian rebellion and formally took over the country from the Company. India became a British colony and Queen Victoria was crowned the first Empress of India. India would remain under British rule until its independence on August 15, 1947.

As a teenager, like many others in Allahabad, I visited the large verdant park in the city, still called Company Gardens, a lingering reminder of the British East India Company. One afternoon while walking in a shaded, overgrown grassy area, I stubbed my toe on Queen Victoria's huge black stone statue, which lay on its side. It had been toppled over by citizens of Allahabad in the surge of emotions when India gained its independence on August 15, 1947. Queen Victoria's face flattened the rough grass on which it lay, far from its ornately carved canopied pedestal. The statue has since been carted away to some unknown destination, but the empty pedestal stands, a stark reminder of a world that once was, and an empire whose sun had finally set.

When I visited my final destination in Gwalior, I thought of that vanquished statue as I stared into the stone face of Lakshmi Bai, her sculpted face resolute, eyes fixed on a distant horizon. Larger than life, she sat on a horse rearing up on its hind legs, informing the viewer that this warrior had died in battle. In one hand, she held up her large sword, the other gripped the reins.

I walked around to the back of the statue and spotted the young boy seated behind her. I turned right, toward the rugged beauty of Gwalior fort atop its hill, shimmering in the dust-haze miles away. On an impulse earlier that morning, I had stopped by a roadside stall that sold long strands of fragrant jasmine flowers and had wound them around my wrist like a bracelet. They were already somewhat wilted. I closed my eyes as I brought my wrist to my nose and inhaled the heady fresh perfume, then unwound the strand from my wrist and placed it at the base of her statue.

Queen Lakshmi Bai of Jhansi was a woman ahead of her time while still firmly astride her own. When I examine her life, she appears as an intriguing mix of traditional and modern. In being both, she expanded the definition of Indian women in general and Indian mothers, in particular. That makes her appeal timeless, which is perhaps why I feel a kinship with her.

Widowhood and the loss of her kingdom didn't deter her from doing what she knew she needed to do. Underneath it all, the source of her strength was her son. She left him with the certain, unshakeable knowledge that his mother loved him more than anything or anyone. What more can a mother do?

Though I am sure I fall short every day, and I hope I never have to make the choices she did, there is one luminous thread that binds me with her across the ages. When all else perishes, love is all that remains, even after death. Lakshmi Bai remains my most enduring inspiration. It is time to move on however, to discover other warrior queens, for life and journeys only have one trajectory: forward.

Chapter Three

History, Tradition, and Rebellion

"I know now I'm well and truly married to the Brigade."
    Begum Sumroo: A Play in Three Acts (Partap Sharma)
    Begum Samru of Sardhana (1778-1837)

On the evening of India's 17th Republic Day, January 26, 1967, in the small town of Meerut, I was born in a building grandiosely named Nadir Ali Shah Palace. It had once been a palace of a minor noble but became the official residence and offices of my father, the then Regional Food Controller of Meerut. It was a huge, crumbling old building, parts of which were in perpetual need of repair.

About twenty miles from Meerut lay the small principality of Sardhana which, in the nineteenth century, was ruled by the quirky and indomitable Begum Samru. Begum can mean lady or, as in her case, the female equivalent of a nawab or minor prince. For most of my childhood and early adulthood, Begum Samru remained mostly a local obscure local legend I had never heard about.

Chapter Three

In my mid-twenties, I came across a short article about her in a magazine and was immediately enchanted. She was a warrior no doubt, but she was the thinking woman's warrior, more stateswoman than soldier, though she had no fear of battle. Begum Samru is the warrior queen that other warrior queens must have aspired to be. Victorious and undefeated, she maintained control of her kingdom and died peacefully in her own bed at a ripe old age.

We moved from Meerut when I was just a few months old. I visited my birthplace when I was ten years old. I remember standing in the painfully florescent-blue room in which I had been born, my parents' bedroom, which had since been reconfigured many times over. A quintessential Indian government office, its walls were lined with tilting towers of dusty files with four mismatched heavy dark wood desks and chairs located at each corner of the room. A large wooden board on which were painted the names of each officer and the years they had spent there hung askew on one wall. In neat white Devnagari, Hindi script, was written, *Mohd. Saidullah, 1964-1967*. I was born in 1967. By April of that same year my father was transferred to the small town of Unnao.

Where had the bed been? Which wall had the wardrobe been placed against? What had become of the mirror which my mother used to apply her lipstick and kohl? My mother was terrified—and rightly so—of hospitals in small Indian towns. There certainly were enough stories of rude nurses, disinterested doctors, and less than sanitary conditions.

Even before homebirths became fashionable and a new age fad in western countries, many women in India gave birth in the comfort of their own homes. As a child, I was embarrassed to have been born at home since all my friends seemed to have been born in "maternity nursing homes," which are small clinics owned by obstetricians. By the time I went to school in the larger town of Allahabad, only poor ignorant women in villages were forced to have homebirths.

Now I stood in the very room in which I was born, attended by a female doctor, a nurse, and our faithful family retainer Shakira khala. The latter was the first to hold me, I am told. Perhaps that is why I felt a special connection with her and looked upon her as a second mother. She was a fixture in our house and worked as cook and housekeeper. Just a week after writing this paragraph, I received news that she had died. Another piece of my childhood excised.

My four siblings often recount how, as my mother labored to birth me, my father talked with them outside while they walked in circles around the giant building. They didn't really understand what was happening until they came in from the cold January evening to be greeted by their squawking newborn sister.

Since there was no other way to get to Sardhana except through Meerut, I decided to visit the city of my birth once again in June 2012. Meerut was also the only nearby town that had lodging for rent. My mother and one of my sisters came with me, which gave us an opportunity to revisit the past together. I saw a mere glimpse of the dilapidated Nadir Ali Shah Palace. It appeared to be sinking into the earth and I wondered that the building remained standing.

The mid 1700's in India was known as *gardi ka waqt* or *the time of the troubles*. Farzana Begum Samru was born and lived during these chaotic times. Little is known about her early life, but we do know her name was Farzana and that she was probably born in 1750. Her mother, a former dancing girl/courtesan named Zeldah, became the concubine of a man named Latafat Khan. Latafat lived in the village of Kutana, barely thirty miles from Sardhana. Farzana's father died in about 1756 when she was six years old. Latafat's senior wife and children appropriated all his property and worldly goods and kicked out his concubine and their half-sister Farzana. Penniless and homeless, Zeldah returned to Shahjahanabad —currently called Old Delhi to distinguish it from the British created New Delhi—the place from which her now-dead patron had acquired her. They met in a *kotha*, a salon where courtesans danced and entertained men, and this is where she returned.

After the death of the last powerful Mughal emperor Aurangzeb in 1707, Shahjahanabad declined into a crumbling city. Since then, waves of invasions from Afghans, Persians, and Marathas further devastated the city that had once been the pride of the Mughal empire. The formidable British East India Company continued to annex kingdom after kingdom through various battles and alliances. The French and Portuguese were still at war with the British, in an effort to seize as much of India—if not all—for themselves. During these times, mercenaries peddled their services to whichever power could afford them.

In the 1750's, Shahjahanabad was also a city mired in child sex trafficking, specializing in the sale of child-virgins. It is not known whether Zeldah sold her daughter or if Farzana came to her fate in some other way. It is definitely known, however, that fourteen-year-old Farzana entertained men in the same ways her mother once had. She too was a courtesan, caught in the shaded area somewhere between dancing girl and prostitute.

At barely four-foot-eight, the young and beautiful Farzana had a reputation for being a temptress. As a young girl, she leveraged the only skills she had to her advantage. A nautch girl like her operated outside the bonds and restrictive rules of polite society, which allowed her independence other women didn't have. She exercised her influence and learned cultured ways, including poetry and the art of charming conversation. In some ways this was preferable to noble and respectable women, mostly kept uneducated and docile, who spent their entire lives confined to their homes, where their fathers and husbands kept them tied to housework and the birthing and raising of children. These women were merely the means by which to propagate bloodlines and dynasties, their names lost to history.

This is where Zeldah crossed paths with Walter Balthazar Reinhardt Sombre, a "morose and ill-conditioned ruffian" with no scruples or conscience. Originally a carpenter from a working-class Austrian family, like other mercenaries, Sombre headed to India to make his fortune. He provided his services to the French and earned the moniker Le Sombre due to his constantly somber expression. Over the years, this was Indianized to Samru. Sombre didn't have the largest mercenary army with three battalions of soldiers, about two hundred horses, a good train of artillery, and fourteen mounted guns. In 1765, General Sombre purchased Farzana for an unknown sum of money. She was fourteen, he was forty-five. Like her mother before her, Farzana became the concubine of a rich man. Unlike her mother, that's not what she remained.

Like Farzana, I was born into a Muslim home. Unlike her, my parents were respectably married and already had four children before I came along. Being solidly and respectably middle class, my parents' lifestyle was diametrically opposed to Farzana's life. Their last child (before me), my brother, was nine when my mother experienced the early symptoms of pregnancy, which a dismissive doctor diagnosed as a tumor. After taking some medications she no longer remembers, she followed her instincts, and I was born a few months later. Not a tumor at all.

Unlike Farzana, who followed in her mother's footsteps, I tried even as a young child to be the exact opposite of my mother. We have a complex relationship, my mother and me. She inducted me into the world of reading and that's an obsession we still share. But her parents married her to my father in an arranged to marry at twenty-one, right after she graduated with a Bachelor's degree in math. My father, twenty-nine and a young officer in the Indian Administrative Service (I.A.S.), entered the life of the spouse of a public servant, which was mainly a ceremonial, supporting role.

For my mother, this meant attending ribbon-cuttings, smiling graciously by the side of her husband, and hosting important dinners and social events at their home. As I write these words, I see now as I never did before the similarities between Begum Samru and my mother. Both were young and left behind the familiar to embrace older men to whom they were bound without their consent.

By the early 1760's, the British defeated the French in India. The French Indian colony shrank to the territory of Pondicherry. The Portuguese were considered no real threat and were mainly concentrated in Goa.

According to the terms of the 1763 Treaty of Paris, the French were to abandon their Indian endeavors. However, the mercenaries who had served the French didn't follow their benefactors back to Europe. There were still fortunes to be made in India with the various small kingdoms and principalities fighting each other, and against foreign invasions from Central Asia and the Maratha incursions from India's Deccan plateau. Le Sombre kept busy fighting for whoever paid him.

Most mercenaries were given sizable *jagirs* or land grants for maintaining their armies and their estates. The French state of the *Doab*, the fertile land between two rivers, had been created by the greatest of all French mercenaries, de Boigne. Samru, however surly and unlikeable, had no such jagir. He traveled where work took him, to the court of whichever prince, king, or chieftain would hire him. The British, however, wouldn't hire him, as compelling evidence indicated that he and his men presided over a massacre of the head of an English factory. He was a hunted by the British and dared not venture outside the United Provinces, now mostly contained in the modern state of Uttar Pradesh. After 1763, Sombre and his army served no less than fourteen masters.

Sombre and his household did not live a lavish life but, like other foreign mercenaries, he adopted Indian ways, including maintaining a harem. He had one concubine called Barri Bibi, who conveniently melted into the shadows when Samru returned with his new vivacious companion, the teenaged Farzana. Barri Bibi, simply called the older lady, had a son, Zafaryab, who was regarded as mentally feeble, though no particulars can be found about what that actually meant. Three other children from that relationship have been lost to history.

Though there is no evidence that Sombre and Farzana were ever married, and despite the existence of other concubines, she always acted and behaved as a legitimate wife. She was the only one known as Samru's begum or Begum Samru even after his death. By the time she died, she was Her Highness the Begum Samru. Farzana joined his traveling life and was known to accompany him on some of his military campaigns. He reportedly taught her, or she leaned by observing, how to run a successful mercenary army. She became his constant companion and Sombre continued to be enchanted by her. She used his proximity to learn everything she could. Samru, his new begum, and the rest of the household followed him wherever his army served. It was an unstable migrant lifestyle.

My mother's family returned to Burma when, in 1947, my grandfather was appointed independent India's first ambassador to the country of his and my mother's birth. His own father had moved to Burma to become a prosperous teak merchant and that is where my mother was born and lived until she turned nine, near the end of World War II. When Japanese bombers started to decimate Burma in 1942, the family fled on the last ship to leave Rangoon harbor. They lived in India as refugees as my grandfather struggled to rebuild his law practice in Allahabad at the High Court.

He succeeded and maintained a friendship born of a common love of books with the Indian leader of the independence movement, Jawahar Lal Nehru. Before Nehru became Prime Minister of India on August 15, 1947, he had already appointed my grandfather as the Ambassador to Burma. At the same time as the Indian tricolor flew for the first time in India, my grandfather M.A. Rauf unfurled the same flag at the Indian embassy in Rangoon.

In 1953, my parents got married in Rangoon and, a few days later, my mother returned to India where she had spent unhappy, deprived years as a war refugee. She especially had unpleasant memories of Allahabad, her new husband's hometown. Her early adult life was as much without agency as had been Farzana's. She had not been sold, as had been Farzana, since she came from an educated, prosperous family with some social prestige. Technically, she wasn't forced into marriage. She was, however, emotionally blackmailed into the union by her mother. Her overwhelming desire to please her parents and to be the best daughter she could be, left her no choice but to capitulate. And so, at twenty-one, with a freshly minted Bachelor's degree in math, she married my twenty-nine year old father who was in the newly established Indian Administrative Service (IAS).

Samru and his household—including his concubines—were stationed in the Mughal fort of Agra, the locus of the diminishing Mughal empire. The Emperor Shah Alam II was an ineffectual head of a dynasty sliding toward ultimate decimation. Many accounts talk about Samru increasingly relying on his new begum. Even at her young age, Farzana was known as a dealmaker and was crucial to making Sombre more successful and stable, which softened his unsociable and somber reputation.

As mercenaries, they reported to Najaf Khan, the *vizier* or the chief noble of the Mughal empire. As payment for his services and to cover the expenses of his troops, Najaf Khan gave Sombre the towns of Panipat and Sonepat. The revenues generated were not enough to maintain his army and his family. He was getting older and tired and wanted to give up the itinerant life of a mercenary and settle down to work for one master.

His young new begum convinced Najaf Khan that their army would permanently protect Mughal interests. For revenue they were given a huge *jagir*, from Aligarh to Muzzafarnagar, one hundred and twenty-two miles away. Farzana selected the village of Sardhana just north-west of Meerut as their headquarters. It was 1776 and Farzana was still in her mid-twenties.

Despite gender, Farzana endeared herself to the old emperor, Shah Alam II, who affectionately called her his "beloved daughter," and bestowed upon her a new name, *Zeb-un-Nissa*, an adornment among women. Clearly, the old mores of segregation by gender and the rules of Mughal etiquette were long gone and Farzana is said to have spent quite a bit of time with the emperor. Gradually, the young woman made herself the de-facto heir to Sombre's army, solidifying her position with their Mughal patrons and displaying her deal-making skills. She was also known to her mercenary soldiers as a decision-maker and leader.

It is noted that Farzana, forever eager to return to the area where she had lived as a child, was the ultimate deal maker for this exchange and that Najaf Khan recognized her as a powerful and loyal ally. Sombre didn't live long enough to enjoy his new prosperity and died suddenly in 1778. He was buried in a nondescript grave now lost in time. A power struggle ensued. Who should assume command of his army? Who would rule Sardhana?

My mother grew up in Allahabad, attended Girls' High School and then went on to Allahabad University. But she felt trapped. Just as I daydream of the Allahabad of my past, painting my hometown in rose-colored tones, so she did with Burma. Burma was magical. She had been happy in Burma as a child, where there were no money issues and no war.

I remember a story she once told me of when she returned to Rangoon after the war. She was most excited to visit a posh shopping area she loved. She spoke of the huge, elegant shops. But she returned to find small squalid stores that had been hastily rebuilt after the war. The golden past too often dissolves under the direct gaze of the present. I experienced the same hollow feeling when I returned to Allahabad—the city now felt like a backwater trap—and measured what was against what is.

With the myopic selfishness of a child, I never considered my mother's perspective because I identified so much with my father. Perhaps because he and I were so alike. I look like my father, the same round face, small hooded-eyes, and snub nose. I also related to him. I wanted to be like him, be him. My father was easy to understand. He was straightforward, simple, and steadfast in his beliefs and values. We were both also equally pig-headed with a very black and white view of right and wrong. Also, like him, I loved the city in which we lived, Allahabad, despite its slow slide into ruin.

Both of us—I thought—were unlike my mother, who was emotionally mercurial, charismatic but manipulative with a more nuanced view of right and wrong. I learned early on not to confide in her because she was likely to use that information during vulnerable times. It was hard to know where I stood with my mother. The same behavior that might make her laugh one day, might lead to a tongue lashing the next. That was, of course, the reason I never told her about my childhood molestation.

Yet, it was my mother who instilled in me a love of reading and travel. And though I strove to escape this reality, I have the same restlessness that she had—has. And it is through my mother that I have a deeper familial connection, not only with Meerut, but with Sardhana. For my mother told stories, stories from our ancestral past of her relatives, dead and alive, long-ago tales of people from other times. Stories are the currency of families and she told me many, weaving me into the fabric of our shared history, whether I appreciated them or not.

As I tell stories of my family to my own daughter, I bind her to me with these tales of events that happened in another time. I realize also that I need to understand my mother, I need to see where we are the same and where we differ. I need to forgive her, as well as myself, and I need to know how she became the person she did and how I became the one I did. If I am to be a good mother, I need to understand my mother. It is time to embrace a more nuanced, grey-shaded worldview without losing my father's tough moral compass.

To me, Begum Samru remains the quintessential outsider who created her own world in which she ruled supreme while others served her. She was a survivor, initially with no agency as she was literally a purchased woman, yet she wrested power and self-respect for herself. She was, like me, an immigrant, born in one place and immigrated to another. That she is identified with the place she made her own is testament to her fortitude, patience, and intelligence.

Those with no first-hand knowledge of immigration might imagine the overwhelming emotions to be a sense of adventure, relief, euphoria even. Being transplanted brought with it none of those feelings for me. The first conscious thought I remember waking up to that first morning in Lexington, Kentucky was, *I don't know anyone here.* A feeling of utter and total isolation swept over me. I arrived in the U.S. in the fall of 1987, before social media, email, and WhatsApp video calls. My major means of communication was the long letters I wrote to friends and family. International phone calls were prohibitively expensive with calls to India around three dollars per minute, so were reserved for emergencies or birthdays.

Once I arrived in my new home, I became effectively marooned. I spoke the language, but I lived in an alien land, was trapped in an alien culture, and I felt alone. More alone than I could have ever imagined. I spent a lot of those early years yearning for my family, a sense of belonging, and sense of history that bound me to the place in which I had lived. I felt dislocated in America. I didn't belong. No unbroken links of history bound me to this place. I was unrooted. "Resident alien," was the technical term at that time, and that is what I felt. I was resident in America, but I was alien to it, and it to me. I then gradually started gathering bits and pieces of my family's past, in an effort to reach back into history and determine where I came from. That view in the rear mirror is crucial before I could look ahead to see where I wanted to go.

The maternal side of my mother's family were wealthy landowners from Meerut. A family mansion still stands somewhere, an ancient crumbling island in the haphazardly booming city growing around it. I tried to locate the home but since I wasn't in Meerut for that long, I let it go. It was time to move on to Sardhana.

One of my mother's maternal aunts married a wealthy nawab of Sardhana. Like all minor princes, he owned a lot of land and property. As a condition of their marriage contract, he transferred a mansion and some land to her so she would have an independent income. During my childhood, I heard of Sardhana only in the context of this great aunt, whom I knew of as Bubani. The husband apparently preferred men and frequently brought home various men he picked up. This didn't stop him from procreating with his legal wife and together they had several children.

His sexual orientation remained a shameful secret, especially from his family. His wife agreed to stay with him until the deaths of his parents, and her and her children's lives continued without interruption. Then his parents died, and he ceased all financial support of her and their children. Eventually, Bubani moved to the newly formed Muslim nation of Pakistan where her son had become a famous movie star in its fledgling film industry. Her story remained my touchpoint with Sardhana, until I discovered Begum Samru in the late 1990's through a short article in a long-forgotten magazine. The begum instantly grabbed my attention and my imagination, even as other endeavors didn't let me investigate her any further. So, my journey there in late 2012 was the culmination of a fascination decades in the making. I couldn't wait to see the little town inextricably linked with the begum.

Sardhana is merely twenty-three miles on a narrow, bumpy road that links it to Meerut. However, the ride took us well over an hour because of the usual Indian road conditions, wandering cattle, slow-moving bicycles, and just the generally low rate of speed over the frequently rutted road, especially when passing through more populated areas.

We crossed a bumpy bridge over the Yamuna River. Barely clothed young boys were swam, splashed around and laughed boisterously, the sights and sounds of an Indian summer. Women and girls washed clothes at the banks of the river, beating the fabric against rocks, cleaning and destroying them simultaneously.

Three years after Sombre's death, in 1781, Farzana converted to Christianity, specifically Catholicism. Father Keegan who authored *Sardhana and its Begum,* writes, *"Three years after the death of her husband, she became a convert to the Catholic Church and was baptized under the name of Joanna, at Agra, on the 7th of May 1781, by the Revd. Fr Gregorio, a Carmelite monk."* Her new name was Joanna Nobilus.

There is little information about whether this was a true spiritual conversion or if her motivations were more practical and worldly. Some biographers hint that she might have converted to honor Sombre's legacy but there is no evidence that the mercenary had been particularly religious. Judging by the practicality of her decisions, I believe honoring Sombre was the main reason for her conversion.

Despite now being Joanna Nobilis, Her Majesty the Begum of Samru, Farzana continued wearing her ornate Mughal-Indian clothes, which included curly-toed shoes and she smoked her ever-present hookah. She embodied duality, one in *purdah* as the sequestered Indian Muslim widow of

Sombre, the other when she would cast off her veil to interact with her men and meet and dine with other Europeans in India. She also established herself as a formidable leader of an able fighting force. The English Colonel Skinner had first seen her as a beautiful young woman at the head of her troops and displaying, even in the heat of battle, calmness, courage, and presence of mind. Later he would write that those *"...who have opportunities of hearing of, and witnessing her exploits, form a series of scenes, such as perhaps no other female could have gone through."*

One of the most pervasive memories I have of my school, St. Mary's Convent, is the dark, cool interior of our small chapel on hot summer days. Next door to our school, separated by an ornate iron fence, sat the large St. Joseph's cathedral in the campus of the boy's school and seminary of the same name. We spied at the boys in their light blue shirts and dark blue trousers when they headed into the cathedral. They looked just as anxious as we felt during those stressful times.

I lived the typical life of a young Indian girl from an upper-middle class, educated family in India. All of us—regardless of religion—were perceived to be good, obedient girls, and all of us were sent to each city's most prestigious schools: Catholic convents for the girls, and schools affiliated with seminaries for the boys. Except for the Catholic kids who had catechism, there was no religious instruction in these schools. While the Catholic kids were at catechism, us non-Catholics imbibed lessons of ethics and morality in Moral Science class. However, before and after classes, we had access to the chapel, the shaded grotto where the virgin Mary stood with the infant Jesus, and on special occasions even the St. Joseph's Cathedral next door. Our corridors were lined with pictures of the holy family and sayings from the Bible were prominently displayed. Eight hours a day, six days a week (we only had Sundays off) for twelve years, this was my environment. I was most comfortable with this setting.

During finals week, in a last-ditch effort to do everything possible to do well, all of us girls—it didn't matter our religious affiliations—flooded the chapel to bargain with God, Jesus, Mary, and the holy spirit for good grades. I remember dipping my fingertips into the holy water and making the sign of the cross, then kneeling on a pew and wishing with all my might that I remembered everything I had studied—or barely studied.

It's funny to think of this now as an atheist and as a nice Muslim girl (with niggling doubts eating away at me). There I was with my giant glasses and two long braids, begging for good grades from a god I didn't believe existed. The ritual was somehow comforting. It was insurance. I had my doubts about God but if s/he did exist, surely my diligent, fervent prayers would help. It's strange that I never did the *namaz* at home to ask Allah for good grades.

Even now, I find comfort and serenity in churches and their rituals. The coolness of the holy water, the calm subdued interior, the flickering candles, the silent prayers of the nuns. In my own self-absorbed way, praying to the holy trinity was my own practical decision to leave no stone unturned in the quest for good grades.

As was the custom of Farzana's time, after Sombre's death, command of his army went to his son Zafaryab. Despite still being in mourning, Begum Samru would not let this happen. She had the support of the troops, who also knew of Zafaryab's lack of intelligence and profligate ways. The begum also had the support of Najaf Khan and the confidence that the emperor regarded her as his daughter.

Perhaps she remembered the sudden upheaval of her childhood and what it was like to lose her home because she did not inflict this fate upon Zafaryab or his mother. She gifted Zafaryab property and funded a luxurious life for him in Delhi, where he immersed himself in poetry and the arts.

The begum became the commander of the four thousand troops she had inherited from Sombre. This included about one hundred European officers and soldiers. She moved to Sardhana, merely thirty miles from Kutana, where she had lived and been exiled from as a child. Farzana, Joanna, Zeb-un-Nissa didn't merely command a mercenary army, she ruled Sardhana.

Flamboyant and unconventional, she held court in Sardhana while wearing a masculine turban and smoking her hookah, but otherwise attired in lavish Mughal attire. When the mood struck her, she would abandon *purdah* and dine with her European officers.

Whatever her campaigns in the past as solo commander of her army, she often led her troops into battle. There are paintings of her at the head of her army, a tiny figure seated atop a magnificently caparisoned elephant. She came to the rescue of Emperor Shah Alam II several times. Skilled though she was as a commander, she truly shone as a deal maker and diplomat.

In 1783, a Sikh army of thirty thousand led by Baghel Singh camped on the outskirts of Delhi. The emperor was terrified, rightly so, of losing his throne, and enlisted Farzana's help. She negotiated with Baghel Singh and persuaded him to withdraw for the relatively cheap price of allowing the Sikhs to build eight gurudwaras in Delhi. They also accepted a percentage of the revenue collected in the empire, but only for that year.

In 1788, the psychopathic Rohilla chieftain Ghulam Qadir occupied Delhi. The Rohillas were a powerful martial tribe originally from Afghanistan. In India, they occupied a large territory named Rohilkhand. There are accounts that Qadir had been captured and tortured by Mughal forces when he was a child. When he captured Delhi, he returned the favor by torturing Shah Alam and personally gouged out the Emperor's eyes.

Begum Samru rushed to aid the Mughals and contemptuously spurned Qadir's offer of marriage and a proposition to share power. Faced with Samru's superior artillery power and forces, Qadir fled Delhi. A while later, he was captured by Mahadaji Shinde, the deputy regent of affairs for the Mughal empire. It is said that his eyeballs were sent to court in a box, so the blind emperor felt them with his fingers.

When I first arrived in the U.S. before I started my studies at the University of Kentucky, things were pretty grim. My mother and I were living with her brother, my uncle, an Emergency Room physician, who owned thirty or so thoroughbreds that either lost most races or were injured. Keeping one horse is a hobby, keeping and breeding dozens is financial ruin, which was to be his sad eventual end. Horse racing bulletin boards still discuss how he was the owner with the most losses, three hundred and thirty-five consecutive races between 1990 and 2007.

However, when he generously invited us to live with him, he had just begun his downward descent, which would take a couple of decades to complete. In the mid-1980's when we arrived, the Indian government only allowed us to take three hundred dollars each out of the country. To contribute to the household and gain some measure of independence I had to find work, and fast.

I had grown up as a typical middleclass Indian kid. We weren't rich but we did have a lot of household help. At the age of nineteen, I had never washed a single dish, cooked, done laundry, or cleaned house. Now I had to do these tasks along with find a job, which in Kentucky in 1987 was no mean feat. There wasn't much to be found, except fast food jobs. I ended up working at Burger King and starting life in a new country at the bottom of the totem pole in my new world taught me lessons I'll always remember.

Now, three decades later, I can't leave a table messy at a fast food restaurant. I know too well that feeling of exhaustion and revulsion when faced with ketchup-stained tables, mashed up French fries, wrappers, and napkins flung about everywhere. I learned lessons in humility when customers spoke to me slowly and painfully as if I was stupid and uneducated, a common stereotype for fast-food workers. I was also a brown Indian girl working in a menial job in the South. For the first time, I had crossed class lines and was doing jobs that I can now acknowledge I then believed were beneath me.

Those were hard times as I established residency in Kentucky, applied to the university, and filled out every financial aid application I could find. Until I was able to be fully absorbed into the relatively liberal welcoming environment of the University of Kentucky, which allowed me to acquire teaching assistantships, my life revolved around working at the restaurant and walking home with the stink of meaty grease permeating every pore of my body. Like most phases in life, this too ended, but the experience left its mark. Each time I look at a young food service worker, I see myself and try to treat them as I would have liked to be treated back then. But I am no saint.

Neither was Begum Samru. There are accounts of her ruthless cruelty. Just four years before her death, two serving women were implicated in a plot to set fire to her houses in Agra, so they could elope with their lovers, soldiers of the guard the begum had left behind. Various accounts exist of her having the women mercilessly flogged.

She was feared as a witch by several smaller chieftains and their people, an impression bolstered by one historical account in which she had the unfortunate women buried alive and then sat atop their premature grave calmly smoking hookah. There were no more reports of any insurrections against her. She had the full trust of her soldiers. And she was no more nor less cruel in her punishments than most rulers of that time.

Despite the shaky start to her life and the manner in which she entered the world of mercenary warfare, once she gained power, maintaining that power became her purpose. Unusual for her time, she was not defined by her relationship with men or family but by what she did. Ironically, even though she took Sombre's name, more people know about her than they do about him. She is the subject of historical exploration while he is a mere footnote associated with her. Despite her romantic dalliances, her focus remained on ruling Sardhana and maintaining her army. She had a laser-like focus on these priorities.

While Sombre had been a man hunted by the British because of the Patna massacre, Begum Samru managed to make allies of them. She did this by using her deal-making abilities and negotiating the release of a British officer held by the Sikhs. Lord Lake, the British Viceroy in India was thoroughly charmed by her, though he scandalized her troops by once greeting her with a kiss.

Begum Samru continued her charm offensive against the British until they decided that she was a valuable ally and confirmed her right to rule Sardhana. Most of her troops were rented out to the British at her expense and her days of being a mercenary leader ended about thirty years before her death around 1800. Begum Samru successfully straddled two important and tricky powerful relationships, both enemies:

the old once-powerful Mughals, and the ascendant British empire.

She shifted her focus fully on to Sardhana itself and raised agricultural yields while lowering rural indebtedness. Within a few years, she raised the revenues from her kingdom many times over. It was during this period of being settled that she began work on the Italian-style basilica that stood in the distance as a signpost to guide my family and I during our drive to Sardhana. The Vincentian architect Antonio Reghelini designed the structure, inspired by St. Peter's in Rome.

My eyes adjusted slowly to the cool darkness as the caretaker opened the large, squeaky doors of the basilica and allowed me into the hall. The voluminous, tall interiors brought relief from the inferno-like heat of the afternoon. Flowers and flickering candles were massed in each of the small chapels and our footsteps echoed on the clean flagstone floors. Only a couple of worshippers prayed silently. Not only had the begum been an enthusiastic Catholic, in her later years, she became a patron of the arts. She was a patron of many artists, writers, and poets, some wonderful, some terrible. Through her able administration, Sardhana became a rich kingdom and she used some of those funds to make it the largest Catholic diocese in North India.

There is an eighteen-foot-tall marble monument of the begum in the basilica. Hand-carved in Italy, the statue was transported by riverboat to Calcutta on the Ganga and finally by bullock cart to Sardhana. The statue depicts the begum in her court. She stands tiny while everyone else carved around her is large. She is already old, her head covered by a diaphanous dupatta, she is dressed in a full skirt and snug *pyjama*. Festooned with jewelry, her prominent rather hooked nose dominates her profile. By her side sits her ever-present hookah, which she holds with one hand. Though hers is the smallest figure amid the crowd of courtiers, she draws the gaze.

The basilica was her crowning glory, and a plaque commemorates her service to the faith. A middle-aged nun appeared, alerted by the caretaker, and crossed herself in the aisle before the altar, then greeted us. She told us some of the history of the basilica and spoke of Begum Samru almost affectionately as if she knew the warrior queen. We walked outside with her, headed for the gift shop that she hinted at. We passed the stations of the cross, larger-than-life white marble statues of Jesus as he trudged to the crucifixion. I looked into his frozen anguished face as the heavy cross made him fall. The extreme pain and sorrow on Mary's face as she beheld her son made me wonder yet, again at how Begum Samru came to her new faith. There are some accounts that Mary herself called the begum.

Begum Samru gave birth to no children. But like so many of the queens who fascinate me, she did have a child, an adopted son. He was the grandson of her stepson Zafaryab who, together with his mother and stepmother, also converted to Catholicism. David Ochterlony Dyce Sombre was the son of Zafaryab's daughter who married the Englishman George Alexander Dyce. The boy's father cared nothing for him, so Begum Samru adopted him after his mother's death.

The begum became a mother late in life when she was close to seventy years old in 1820. She added Ochterlony onto David Dyce's name as homage to her former lover, and Sombre to honor his grandfather, which bolstered his case for inheritance. She wanted to ensure that her son would inherit Sardhana in its entirety.

But, as with Lakshmi Bai, that was not to be. Begum Samru died in 1896 at age ninety, by which time the British had already enacted the Doctrine of Lapse. As expected, they rejected his claim to Sardhana because he was not her direct blood heir, even though, ironically, he was of Sombre's blood. Eventually, David Ochterlony Dyce Sombre left India and traveled the world as an adventurer, though he did return to his mother's bedside when she took ill.

The begum had no choice but to trust the British. It's unclear if she was aware of the implications of the doctrine that wrested away kingdoms from so many adopted children in nineteenth century India. She died, certain that her son would inherit Sardhana and her army. This was not unsurprising because, unlike other royal sons, Dyce Sombre did descend from Reinhardt Sombre, the original ruler of Sardhana. However, since Begum Samru made him *her* heir and there was no blood relationship between them, Sardhana was lost to him. Sardhana rose to prominence with Begum Samru and fell back into obscurity after her death.

Sardhana was one of the richest small kingdoms in British India. In 1953, the begum's fortune was estimated to be around eighteen billion Deutsche Marks. Her fortune has continued to multiply and is contested and unclaimed to this day. Like other warrior queens, Begum Samru was single-minded, ambitious, immensely practical, intelligent and resourceful, even ruthless.

Though she is remembered as a dashing and romantic figure at the head of her army, her strengths were mainly as a deal maker and a master negotiator. Through her wit, intelligence, and charm, she made allies of enemies, recasting Sardhana into a prosperous kingdom with a contented populace that loved her. More importantly, she died at a ripe old age, peacefully in her bed, surrounded by David Ochterlony Dyce Sombre and some trusted courtiers.

As I write this chapter in the winter of 2016, my baby is a

happy three-year-old toddler in pre-school. I wonder at the relationship between Begum Samru and David. There are few details available, but most sources merely say she brought him up as her own. It's redolent with meaning, that phrase, *as her own*. As my daughter climbs all over me and plants an open-mouthed wet kiss on my cheek, I don't feel *as if* she is my own. She is my own simply because she is. Is that how Begum Samru felt about David?

Grandson of the man who purchased her like cattle, named by her for another man she loved. And yet, this boy, this man, was the real love of her life, imbued not just with love but all her hopes for the future. We nurture our children, knowing that most of their lives will not include us. And yet we devote our lives to caring for them. As an older mother, I know that when my daughter is my age I will most likely be long gone. But I think of her future, I wish her a happy and contented life, and that gives me a bitter-sweet satisfaction.

I think back to the final adoption hearing in April 2013, when our baby was just about four months old. We were in Massachusetts while the judge and attorney were in the Midwest where our journey began. I learned that family courts schedule adoption hearings for the end of day. Exhausted from heart-breaking, sad cases of neglect and abuse that fill most of their docket, the court officers, attorneys, and judges like to end their days on a happy, hopeful note.

This was before the days of Zoom court hearings, so we were on a three-way phone call. The ceremony was simple. We essentially swore an oath that there would be no difference between our adopted child and any other children we might have now or in the future. This meant all rights, including that of property. How simply and effortlessly I acknowledged that right. A child's right to inherit from their parents is a basic right. Yet warrior queens died fighting for the right of their children to inherit—most without being able to safeguard that right.

The judge and the attorney congratulated our now legal little family and thanked us for making the end of their day so happy. We went downstairs to where an adoring grandmother held and fed our child. I knelt beside them and kissed my daughter's tiny forehead and cheeks. Her dad did the same. Her grandmother continued feeding her with happy tears in her eyes and she, too, kissed her. The baby, her tummy full, was milk drunk. Her eyelids fluttered in a slowing rhythm before finally closing in a contented sleep.

Chapter Four

Rising from the Rubble

"Answer now, and if fight you won't, I shall negotiate with the English to spare my life." Begum Hazrat Mahal.
   Begum Hazrat Mahal of Lucknow (1857-1858)

Childhood trips to Lucknow were incomplete without a visit to the bustling and vibrant Hazratganj market. Delicate outfits of intricate shadow-embroidery called *chikankari* enticed shoppers with their sorbet-colored shades. Saris, salwar suits, dresses, and tablecloths competed for attention, each store displaying their own particular styles. Much like Lucknow itself, chikankari is elegant, not flashy, white thread worked in intricately exquisite patterns on light-weight cottons and voiles. The city's best-known export echoes its gentility, breeding, and understated style.

I love the one hundred-and-seventy-five-mile trip from Allahabad to Lucknow. Lucknow was the capital of our state Uttar Pradesh and is filled with fantastic fairytale structures. The city has a history of debauched but genteel kings, insurrection, victory, defeat, and escape, not to mention a lavish and refined food culture.

The heart of Lucknow beats in Hazratganj. As a child, I didn't care about chikankari clothes. However, I would harass my mother until she bought me intricate bejeweled *bindis*. These were not the flat plastic stick-ons but were tiny pieces of jewelry themselves. I remember painting the back of bindis with brown glue, then carefully centering them in the middle of my forehead just between my eyebrows. I loved the mini tassel of fake seed pearls that swished from the tear drop shaped ornament. Invariably, I'd lose them soon after, which led to many tantrums and tears. One day, I promised myself I'd go back and buy hundreds of them, so I would never be without one. However, the ultimate legacy of Lucknow became not my beloved bindis but the name of the market itself, or rather the woman for whom the city was named, Begum Hazrat Mahal.

In the summer of 2012, I returned to Lucknow in an attempt to place its one-time queen and commander within its boundaries. Begum Hazrat Mahal comes alive in Lucknow as in no other place. Like most, I considered her a footnote to history, an insignificant player in the power struggle between the British and the fading kingdom of Awadh. That is how she is presented in many history books. During one short visit to Lucknow in the early 2000's, my taxi passed through an old city gate, ornamented by the sinuous curved fish symbol of the Awadh empire. Lucknow had been the capital of the state of Awadh and the jewel in its crown.

"Can you imagine, madam, Hazrat Mahal Begum rode through here, leading her army?" the taxi driver told me.

I imagined her, astride her horse, long curly hair loose around her face, skin dark and lustrous. That hazily romantic image pasted itself upon the picture I already had of this woman, this queen, this rebel, and stayed with me as I ferreted out information from various mentions of her in works about the 1857 mutiny and Lucknow and Awadh.

Hazrat Mahal Begum was born Muhammadi Khanum to a slave of African origin and her unknown lover. Details of her early life remain murky, but it is known that sometime during her adolescence she was sold to a brothel. Being a courtesan in a city renowned for its beautiful, cultured courtesans was the best to which an impoverished girl could aspire. Wealthy and noble families sent their sons to courtesans to learn sophisticated manners and speech. The Awadh into which the young courtesan plied her trade was a kingdom in decline.

In the Battle of Buxar in 1764, the Calcutta based East India Company decisively defeated the weakened Mughal forces and their allies, the nawabs of Bengal and of Awadh. Awadh was a rich and prosperous kingdom and, as part of the Treaty of Allahabad that marked their victory, the British appointed themselves Regents of Lucknow. Awadh was now the treasury that bankrolled the Company and their various campaigns. The British East India Company administered states like Awadh through their Residents.

Residents were senior British officers posted in princely states. The job was technically diplomatic in nature, but they were primarily there to ensure that the rulers strictly upheld their alliances with the British. So, essentially, they were posted to states not formally administered by or under the control of the British. These Residents wielded great power but, since they weren't rulers, they had little responsibility. They were, however, responsible for ensuring that the Company's coffers were filled as the Company gradually undermined the rulers in preparation for taking over those states.

The last nawab of Awadh was Wajid Ali Shah, who was often ridiculed as a drunken louche interested only in writing and performing in plays. He also spent most of his time with his harem in his *Pari Khana* or Garden of Fairies.

As a young nawab, Wajid Ali Shah had plans to improve the lives of his populace. After ascending the throne in 1847, he lobbied to have telegraph made available in Lucknow and tried to organize the Awadhi army into discrete regiments. He also planned and laid the foundations for various public works. However, armed with the terms of the Treaty of Allahabad, the Resident vetoed all his plans and diverted funds ear-marked for these projects into the Company's coffers instead. The Resident was guarded and supported by soldiers loyal to the British but paid from the Awadh treasury.

Eventually, like his predecessors, the nawab retreated from governance altogether, and devoted himself to art. He is famous for having created the energetic and graceful dance form of *kathak* and wrote several plays. The nawab would play Lord Krishna with his maidens around him.

A prolific romantic, Wajid Ali Shah fell in love with regularity, despite having several wives of noble birth with important political connections. Political connections that proved to be futile because of the ubiquitous presence of the Resident who represented the might of the British empire. The nawab surrounded himself with women, hundreds of courtesans, palanquin bearers, domestic servants, or really, any woman who took his fancy. Unlike the usual Indian preference for light skin, he was attracted to dark-skinned women. That is how the young courtesan Muhammadi Khanum came to be one of his "fairies," a member of his huge harem. This is estimated to have been in the early to mid-1840's.

The new fairy was renamed Mehak Pari (fragrant fairy). She is depicted in a painting, beautiful and unashamedly dark-skinned. In the portrait, she is wearing wide, pleated trousers, a tight, short blouse, and a diaphanous dupatta. By all accounts, the nawab was completely enamored of his new mistress for a while and wrote many poems about and for her.

In 1845, she became pregnant and had a son named Birjis Qadr. Bearing the ruler's son elevated her status. She was no longer just an ordinary fairy, nor merely a courtesan. Giving birth to the nawab's son set her apart. She gained privileges such as the right to veil her face and was renamed Iftikhar-un-Nissa (Dignified Among Women).

She also gained her own household, complete with guards, servants and slaves, and an impressive annual kingdom of about Rs. 12,000 a year. She acquired beautiful jewelry and clothes and dined on meals almost as sumptuous as Wajid Ali Shah himself. By 1850, however, he severed his relationship with her, probably because the queen mother abhorred her because of her low-born status and perhaps even her dark skin. In fact, the queen mother was known for instigating divorces and separations from all of the low-born wives and concubines. Despite the end of her relationship with the nawab, Hazrat Mahal's status remained secure. Since she was no longer a formal part of the nawab's inner circle, Hazrat Mahal and her son Birjis Qadr moved from the palace compound to a house in the city. She was happy to retain her income and other perks.

In a strange way, Hazrat Mahal connected me with my mother. As I excavated my memories, this realization surprised me. I always felt a natural kinship with my father and though I loved my mother, we had a troubled and more complex relationship. Yet I discovered that I associated Hazrat Mahal with her. In 1989, I came across a magazine article about a tiny mosque in Lucknow entirely adorned with tiny mirrors. My mother remembered visiting the mosque years earlier but couldn't remember the address or how to get there. This was, of course, before the web made everything easy to find. On impulse. we decided to travel to Lucknow to see if we could find the mosque. That trip remains one of my best memories of my mother during my young adulthood. We were fellow adventurers, off to solve a mystery, and I felt a sense of kinship and rightness during that brief interlude.

We took the early morning train to Lucknow that summer day. The sun rose lazily over fields heavy with grain, not quite ready for harvest. We arrived late morning, and the next couple of days we rattled around, perched atop cycle rickshaws that tried in vain to dodge potholes on the busy roads. Eventually, close to the time of the evening prayers on the second day, after asking endless people if they knew of the mosque, we finally found it. Modestly white on the exterior, the interior was an explosion of exquisite mirror work. From its Arabic calligraphy to its elaborate geometric adornments, every inch of the mosque was made from tiny colored pieces of glass. Though I remember thinking the building striking, today I barely remember it. That's because mission accomplished, on the third day, a whim led us to the Lucknow Residency.

The British Resident had lived in the huge complex with his entourage. British civilians and military personnel also sheltered there during the siege of Lucknow. The pockmarked, cannon-blasted buildings, most with missing roofs, some without at least one wall, immediately captured my imagination. When I connected the sparse dots of the history of Lucknow, I knew all connections led to Begum Hazrat Mahal. And she led to my mother.

That trip to Lucknow became fossilized as a charmed time, a wonderful memory of my mother. I didn't think about my molestation or the emotional rollercoaster I was usually on with her. I didn't feel gaslit. The time is just a pleasant memory that has made me review and examine our relationship.

It took a few years and many false starts to uncover enough research about Begum Hazrat Mahal to create a fuller flesh and blood image of the woman herself. When I embarked on the journey toward writing this book, I knew Hazrat Mahal had to be a part of my story.

Like Raziya Sultan, she was a Muslim woman, and like Begum Samru she started life as a courtesan and became a queen and a leader. Unlike either of these women, however, she had no father who trained her to be a ruler, nor a besotted benefactor/husband who taught her and let her assume power and responsibility.

The mutiny of 1857 spread rapidly through India, but by early 1858 had begun to dissipate. The superior strength and organization of the British military wore down the rebellion, their well-organized army decimating entire villages and towns in retaliation for their complicity with the rebellion. There are accounts of trees full of corpses hanging from branches in the countryside.

In Lucknow, the Company used the revolt as an excuse to finally and formally oust and exile Wajid Ali Shah. Within five weeks, he left Awadh with his personal possessions and three of his wives. Despite his hamstrung and therefore ineffectual rule, he was popular among his people and was known to be generous and kind. There were accounts of his heartbroken subjects following his entourage to Kanpur, a distance of about sixty miles. The people mourned the end of his rule and the dying of an era that would never return. Wajid Ali Shah instructed his people to obey the laws of the British.

Hazrat Mahal and her son were too unimportant to

accompany the nawab into exile, as were many other wives and concubines. They were abandoned and alone in a city held by the British with a fomenting rebellion in the countryside. On July 3, 1857, Begum Hazrat Mahal stepped into the vacuum created by the sudden removal of the nawab in a city that resented the British and had a need to join the mutiny. She organized a grand procession in the Kaiserbagh Palace and led her son, fourteen-year-old Birjis Qadr, to his coronation as the next nawab of Awadh. The other wives and concubines agreed to Birjis Qadr becoming the visible symbol of Awadh's resistance under the guidance of his mother. She essentially became the ruler of Lucknow.

The British considered the coronation merely an absurd gesture of defiance but to the tattered fringe royal family and the people of Lucknow it was a very real ceremony. The young nawab was crowned with a simple silk turban decorated with gold thread. This was a far cry from the Awadh of even a few weeks earlier. The vast royal treasury, including the crown jewels, other various pieces of jewelry, and weapons had been seized by the Resident.

Worlds and lives can change in an instant just as they did during the pandemic of 2020. The invisible yet deadly presence of COVID-19 has made my now eight-year-old daughter anxious and scared. The sudden catastrophic nature of the pandemic and the subsequent lockdown has rocked her sense of safety. Complicating the scenario for her was that at the end of July 2020 we moved to Germany. Suddenly, everything changed in her world, including a new school.

Talking about the fear helps because she's the kind of kid who needs to work through things. At her International School, she learned that children all over the world face the same challenges she does, and some are in far worse situations. One day, as we spoke in October of 2020, we drove past the small refugee camp in our town. We watched three kids walking into the gate and I pointed them out to her. She already knew about the camp but hadn't paid attention to the fact that some of the refugees were children. That struck her deeply.

She asked about situations that might lead to the sudden and drastic disruption of someone's life. I gently broached the subjects of war and unrest and I found myself telling her about my own mother, who was forced to flee her home in Burma at age eight to live as a refugee in India until the end of World War II. My daughter decided she needed to hear about this from her grandmother herself. Like my daughter, how I wished I could go straight to the source and speak with Hazrat Mahal.

Wajid Ali Shah's exile left a void in Awadh, specifically Lucknow. Suddenly, a kingdom and an administration almost one hundred and fifty years old had crumbled. No one in Lucknow remembered or knew another way of life. The British who had taken over hadn't established another system, partly due to the chaos of the mutiny. No one from the royal family or any other prominent family was likely to resist the British. They probably didn't think that a discarded mistress of the nawab was about to step into the vacuum.

She did so flagrantly and with style. On July 5, 1857, Hazrat Mahal held the formal coronation of Birjis Qadr, and took over as the ruler of Awadh and commander of the rebel forces. She took command of the resistance by staking her son's claim to the throne. The tumult and uncertainty brought about by the exile of the nawab and the ongoing revolt made people yearn for order, structure, and someone to follow. Hazrat Mahal must have recognized the populace's need for stability. It's reasonable to assume that some amount of personal ambition also came into play. There was another reason, a reason common to many of the warrior queens: safeguarding her son's legacy.

While most other warrior queens fought for the rights of their adopted sons, Hazrat Mahal took on the British to secure the rights of her son who, though illegitimate, was the acknowledged son of Wajid Ali Shah, the last nawab of Awadh. If the royal family hadn't been exiled, Birjis Qadr would never have sat on the throne, nor would Hazrat Mahal have been regent. With the nawab and his legitimate children and wives gone, Begum Hazrat Mahal hoped to safeguard the kingdom of Awadh and her son's rightful place as the new ruler.

On a video call one evening, my daughter asked my mother for the details about her childhood experiences of World War II. My mother told her of being evacuated from Rangoon to their farmhouse in the country. Leaving might not have seemed the smartest decision because their village was close to the border and Japanese bombers would drop all their unused payload over the countryside on their way back. Sure enough, a few days after their arrival, the farmhouse was directly hit and obliterated.

The family returned to Rangoon as the war ratcheted up and bombings grew more frequent. The family of five children and two parents grew instantly to include five more kids from the now-destroyed local orphanage. No relatives had come forward to claim these children and the administration appealed to my grandparents for help. They unofficially adopted the five young children. Meanwhile, Japanese bombers continued to rain their deadly cargo on the populace, and kamikaze pilots targeted shelters where people were likely to congregate.

The family, now composed of twelve souls, decided to flee to Burma. They were to leave the very day they decided upon this course of action. They could only take two suitcases for the twelve of them. My mother remembers she and her siblings trying to sneak their toys into the suitcases. They were unsuccessful and my mother was forced to leave behind her impressive doll collection.

The family finished dinner, left the table set as it was, gathered whatever cash they could scrounge together—the banks were closed—then closed the door and departed.

I listened to daughter and grandmother debate the likelihood of carrying at least one toy if necessary. Finally, my daughter said, "Grandma I don't like dolls. I think they are creepy, but I am so sorry you had to leave your dolls behind." I witnessed my almost ninety-year-old mother and my eight-year-old daughter forge a bond across generations, bypassing me. They did it through stories, for stories bind families. My mother and I shared stories too, but we also had an uneasy history. These days, I seem to remember the stories more than the history. Life circles upon itself sometimes. In forming a circle that spans decades, my mother and my daughter placed me in the middle.

Whatever my issues with my mother, I know she loves my daughter unreservedly and that goes a long way in my book. I have watched them bond, mostly long distance these days. I'm fiercely protective of my child and, like the warrior queens, I want her to have everything she deserves by right.

By July 1857, seven thousand rebel soldiers who had once worked for the East India Company flooded Lucknow. Added to the influx of these soldiers were the eighty-seven thousand employees (including soldiers) that Wajid Ali Shah had been forced to disband before his departure. All of them, including the landed gentry whose forts had been demolished by the British, congregated in Lucknow. They were angry, confused, and hungry for a purpose and a leader.

Begum Hazrat Mahal established a court over which she presided. Huge crowds arrived at the court, accompanied by the unhappy and saddened Awadhi peasants, as well as the citizens of Lucknow. Birjis Qadr's new status, especially with Hazrat Mahal at the helm, gave them a sense of comforting structure and a symbol of the kingdom of Awadh and even the Mughal empire. All these people rallied behind this new incarnation of the kingdom of Awadh.

From that summer of 1857 until March of 1858 when the British seized control of Awadh, Begum Hazrat Mahal was the head of operations in Lucknow. She mounted a siege of the Residency, essentially trapping about three thousand British civilians and army personnel, including the Resident and his household.

July of 2012, after more than twenty-five years, I once again walked through ruins of the thirty-three-acre Residency compound. The buildings were as I remembered, as they had been left in 1858. The mutiny had spread to Lucknow and the influx of trained soldiers, and the disgruntled citizenry rallied behind Begum Hazrat Mahal. They responded to her focus and resolve and, by crowning her son as the new nawab, she had legitimacy as his guardian and regent. The most visible symbol of British hegemony in Awadh was the Residency of Lucknow.

Therefore, on June 30, 1857, under her leadership, angry rebel forces surrounded the Residency compound. British commander Sir Henry Lawrence had failed to secure the help of influential landed gentry of Awadh. It was evident that this was no longer just a *sepoy* (soldier) revolt but a rebellion that had the support of vast swathes of the population. Protective trenches were dug around the Residency and, after a defeat in battle by the rebels, Lawrence retreated to the Residency, which also sheltered other

British civilians and army personnel. Believing themselves to be in mortal danger, the British blew up the magazine and fort housed in a building called *Machhi Bhawan* (Fish Mansion). This was mainly to prevent the rebels from using to their advantage the tunnels underneath the *Machhi Bhawan*.

The rebel army relied on ceaseless and heavy bombardments into the Residency compound. Snipers were posted atop buildings close to the perimeter of the compound. One of the more colorful characters was an African eunuch, once part of Wajid Ali Shah's court and now the rebellion's most successful sniper. The British nicknamed him "Bob the Nailer," and he consistently and unerringly killed at least three targets a day. British casualties began to mount, with Sir Henry Lawrence being one of the first, killed by a cannon ball.

I touched a crumbling wall, gingerly edging toward a huge opening clearly made by a long-ago cannon blast. No building in the Residency escaped destruction. The roofs had been completely destroyed. Mounds of rubble lay in piles, undisturbed for over a century and a half. Despite the searing heat, the rubble was covered by hardy stalks of grass, giving the impression of gentle hillocks.

The bejeweled t-straps of my sandals left faint tan lines on the deeply tanned tops of my feet. I wore these tangible reminders of my visit for over a year. I remember staring at my feet each time I fed my newborn daughter. And each time I thought of Begum Hazrat Mahal and her legacy.

Any walls still standing in the Residency compound were heavily pockmarked by the artillery bombardment. Cannon balls had blown out huge chunks. The Residency house itself, once huge and grand as shown in drawings and paintings, now stood as it had been left at the end of the rebellion, battered, and blown apart. I entered a huge room that might have been a ballroom and my feet crunched on dusty rubble and grass roughened by the summer sun.

To one side, the bare remains of a wall led to another wing of the palatial home. A young courting couple sat on the exposed second floor, hushed giggles and furtive kisses imparting a sense of urgency and passion in the air. Almost everywhere I wandered in the compound I stumbled across sets of young lovers. I wasn't surprised. Places like these allow for privacy, away from disapproving family and society. I smiled and walked away.

With Begum Hazrat Mahal directing the siege, the rebels repulsed British relief forces. During the almost four-and-a-half-month siege, close to half of Lucknow's British population were killed or ran away. Historian William Howard Russell was impressed by Hazrat Mahal and wrote, *"This Begum exhibits great energy and ability."*

On behalf of her son, Hazrat Mahal issued regular proclamations. However, she even made some in her own name, not relying on just the legitimacy of the young nawab. To cement her authority even further, she had coins struck with her name and likeness. To do so in the middle of a chaotic and tumultuous time of war illustrates that she was comfortable with power and unafraid to stake her claim and publicly demonstrate her authority. In one proclamation, she exhorted her followers to stay on course and to fight, for the good times of old were sure to return with their victory.

She declared, *"Therefore exhibit your bravery. God willing you will be endowed with jagirs and rewards even better than in the old days."*

In September 1857, a small British relief force entered the Residency, though they were unable to retake the compound. By this time, however, Delhi, the capital of India and the epicenter of the rebellion, had fallen. The figurehead of the

Chapter Four

rebellion, the aged Mughal Emperor Bahadur Shah Zafar had been dethroned and captured, and his sons publicly beheaded. Zafar was exiled to Burma. Rebels fleeing the carnage in Delhi flooded into Awadh, making it and Lucknow in particular, the new power center of the rebellion. That an actual member of royalty—no matter how far removed—led a sustained resistance lent Lucknow a certain legitimacy in the eyes of the rebels. Energized, Hazrat Mahal called upon all Awadhis to fight in the name of god and continued her struggle with enthusiasm.

By November a contingent of British forces had managed to evacuate the Residency, which infused the rebels with even more fervor. They perceived this as the British having retreated. However, by December of 1857, it became evident that this was far from true. The British were systematically retaking lost towns and villages with extreme violence. Colonel James Neill, a ruthless British officer, became infamous and feared for his "hanging parties." Records were being set for the number of people hanged from the mango trees in the countryside. Instead of tables or stools, he used elephants for the drops. My own hometown of Allahabad was set on fire and Delhi was a site of murderous vengeance fury.

I always thought of these events as being far back in history, ancient almost. When I do the math, I'm shocked to realize that my mother was born in Burma in 1931, barely sixty-nine years after the death of the exiled and indigent Emperor Bahadur Shah Zafar in1862. He died in Burma and was buried in an unmarked grave.

In 1942, my mother and her family boarded the last boat to leave the harbor of Rangoon and arrive safely at its destination. Every vessel that left Rangoon harbor after they did was bombed and sunk. Their ship survived because the captain made the decision to hug the coastline from Burma to

India, bringing its human cargo to safety. This included my eight-year-old mother, her parents, six younger siblings, five newly adopted siblings and two-family retainers. The family went from being part of the prosperous upper crust of society in Burma to being virtually penniless refugees, dependent on any help they could get.

They eventually departed Calcutta for Allahabad. This would be their home for the next few years. Staying in Allahabad made sense. My grandfather's family hailed from a village called Kesaria just outside the city limits. My grandmother's eldest sister, the rich wife of a successful criminal lawyer, also lived there. Most importantly, Allahabad was—and still is—home to the High Court of the state and, given that my grandfather was an Oxford-educated barrister, it was the logical base to restart a legal practice.

For my mother, Allahabad symbolized deprivation, and compared unfavorably to the hazily remembered fairy-tale-like perfection of Rangoon. Instead of being chauffeured to school as she had been in Rangoon, she was forced to walk to school in the searing summer heat. From living in a beautiful home in Burma to making do in dingy ramshackle rented houses. From eating expensive imported biscuits from Europe to mounds of cheap chickpea fritters as after-school snacks. To this day, my mother abhors *pakoras*.

Back in 1857, the rebellion arrived at an impasse. Hazrat Mahal led her troops, an impressive figure atop her elephant. They were now intent on to retaking the stubborn British stronghold of Alambagh, a small palace to the south of Lucknow. The begum realized that there was no hope of succor from any quarter because all other centers of the revolt had been subdued. The rebellion was in shambles and the rebels were on the run in most other territories. Hazrat Mahal came to the realization that the focus of the British forces would be on Awadh, Birjis Qadr, and herself. Treacherous threats from among the factions that comprised her army also arose, plaguing her and dividing her attention.

For a while, the begum and her forces were able to hold firm against both the British and the internal threats. This couldn't last, however. By January of 1858, these double-sided skirmishes depleted the efforts and energies of the Awadhi forces.

Then came news that the British forces, having tamped down the revolt in other strongholds, were headed toward Awadh. Unlike Delhi, Lucknow was an easy target since it was not a walled city. In an effort to rectify this, Hazrat Mahal tried her best, even selling off her personal jewelry, to finance fortifications for the city. Though the British were surprised and impressed by her efforts, the hastily built protective stockades and parapets would prove no match against the British army. The threat against Awadh became even more terrifying when news came that the dreaded Gurkha contingent of the British army—fierce Nepali warriors—were advancing toward Lucknow. Fear of the Gurkhas led to large-scale desertions.

In February 1858, Hazrat Mahal was deserted by an important ally and faced the prospect of a sixty-thousand-strong British army headed toward them, including a contingent brought from Europe to quell the rebellion. Hazrat Mahal's stronghold Kaiserbagh was the last to fall. Russell, a contemporary British diarist, compared Hazrat Mahal to mythical Amazonian warriors. He describes her thus, *"The begum alone stands, this black Semiramide—ardent, intriguing, subtle, courageous, devoted to her son."* Yet, unlike many other Indian warrior queens, Begum Hazrat Mahal was not prepared to die in battle if she could avoid it. She was a survivor.

Though my father was born and brought up in Allahabad, his and my mother's family never crossed paths. As my hometown, every alleyway and obscure place in Allahabad is redolent with memories. As a child, I remember being furious when my mother complained about the city. It was dirty, it was too hot, its people too intrusive and provincial—she hated it. She wasn't wrong in her assessments but to my father and to us children, it was home. Allahabad's mythical, literary, and historical significance elevated the city above any prosaic worldly shortcomings. Only recently have I come to realize and empathize with the reasons for my mother's hatred for the city I loved.

How could she love the place? Her memories are of relatives mocking their straitened circumstances, where she had to do without, where she saw her beloved aristocratic father reduced to riding an old, borrowed bicycle to work, where money was always scarce, and stress was ever-present. Being a refugee is an experience balanced atop the existing trauma of war. Being a refugee is about surviving day to day, life is put on hold.

By 1947, my grandfather had established a decent practice and rekindled his friendship with India's soon-to-be Prime Minister Jawahar Lal Nehru, its first as an independent nation. He opted for Indian citizenship, instead of Burmese, and was appointed by Nehru to be India's first Ambassador to the country of his birth, Burma. On the first morning of independent India on August 15, 1947, my grandfather unfurled the Indian tricolor flag atop the Indian embassy in Rangoon. The family had returned home. They had survived the war, survived their years of deprivation in India and made it back home in an almost cinematically triumphant manner, economic and social prestige restored, even exceeded. My mother recalls that return with the excitement of the teenager she had been.

When I was a child and my mother talked of her childhood during the war, I always saw her as she was, a grown woman in the present, not as the child she had been. Logically, I knew this wasn't accurate, but I didn't really see or feel the difference. My view was obscured. Perhaps this was because of my complex, complicated, often uneasy relationship with her. On one hand, we shared a love of reading, had a similar restlessness, a love of travel, and an aversion to being trapped in one place.

On the other hand, she had a mercurial temper, so I never knew what might set her off. Her old-fashioned belief that children were not to be believed even if they complained about being bullied or abused taught me not to confide in her not just because I knew she wouldn't believe me, but because I knew that the information might be used against me at some later date. This dichotomy meant she erratically careened between egging me on to be a fearless and independent feminist, and berating me for not being an obedient, meek, good, unquestioning religious Muslim girl. I didn't trust her, and she didn't know me. Now I know that I also didn't understand her. I didn't recognize that her beliefs and behaviors emerged from a past made brittle and painful with trauma and dislocation.

I think of her now as a child survivor of war and a victim of untreated PTSD. She is close to ninety years old and, in her, I see reflections of my eight-year-old daughter. My eight-year-old who was able to reach through time, through trauma and generations to empathize with her grandmother taught me to do the same.

Life comes full circle in different ways. We often repeat the actions that are familiar to us and relive the decisions of our ancestors. Even if we try and escape the legacies of our collective and individual pasts, their ghostly fingers reach into our present and even our future, trapping us like flies in honey. It takes an act of conscious will to break away from old, destructive patterns. Consciously breaking through these established patterns offers escape and success is victory even if it's temporary. For nothing lasts forever, neither failure nor victory.

As Hazrat Mahal learned. She had several opportunities to surrender with honor when the British issued the Awadh Proclamation in March 1858. This was essentially an offer of amnesty and guaranteed that those who surrendered would be safe, their rights restored. In return, they would just have to accept the legitimacy and supremacy of the British government. Hazrat Mahal continued fighting and eventually retreated to Baundi Fort near the border of Nepal. From there, she continued to run a sort of shadow-government of Awadh. She collected taxes and revenues, dispensed justice, headed councils of war and issued proclamations. This state-of-affairs continued for close to a year.

Baundi Fort became the symbolic rebel outpost and Hazrat Mahal was joined by Nana Sahib, the Maratha leader who had been on the run after the defeat of his forces and the death of his strongest ally, Rani Lakshmi Bai. At this point, Hazrat Mahal still commanded an army of close to sixteen thousand, including a camel cavalry and about sixteen or seventeen large guns.

Hazrat Mahal remained defiant, especially when, in November 1858, Queen Victoria—the British crown now having taken over India from the British East India Company—issued a proclamation. The Queen promised her "native princes" the right of safety and religious freedom.

In response, Begum Hazrat Mahal issued a counter-proclamation of her own. By doing so, she established that she too was a queen, that she and Victoria were equals. She directly challenged Queen Victoria's promises and assertions.

She stated, *"The rebellion began with religion and for it, millions of men have been killed. Let not our subjects be deceived: thousands were deprived of their religion in the North-West and thousands were hanged rather than abandon their religions."*

Not only was she asserting her own royal status and right to rule by questioning Queen Victoria, Begum Hazrat Mahal was also stating the truth, ensuring that the citizens of Awadh knew what was really going on, despite British promises. Already, Brigadier Napier was converting Awadh's mosques and Muslim shrines into barracks and the communal Friday prayers had been banned.

Begum Hazrat Mahal continued to be an outspoken critic and a thorn in the British's side by publicly listing the landowners and rajas who had lost their ancestral lands and properties—despite Victoria's assertions to the contrary. Begum Hazrat Mahal highlighted the vast amounts of money the British had bled from the kingdom of Awadh over the decades. She openly pointed out that the populace of Awadh remained loyal to its ruling family, which meant the nawab could not have been truly as incompetent as painted by the British. She stated that no other ruler had ever experienced as much loyalty and devotion as she had. *"What then is wanting, that they do not restore our country?"*

Despite her defense of him, Wajid Ali Shah was horrified by his erstwhile begum's unbecoming and unwomanly activities. He publicly denounced her, declaring that both she and Birjis Qadr meant nothing to him and were to have no association with him. Shah continued living in exile, cementing his legacy as a coward. Even now in Awadh, he is compared unfavorably to his martial begum. She is a heroine; he is a weakling, despite his contributions to art and culture.

The inevitable happened. The might of the British empire—not merely the East India Company—was concentrated against the rebel stragglers. When it became clear that defeat was imminent, Hazrat Mahal and her entourage crossed the border on some unknown date in 1858 and sought refuge in Nepal. She would spend the rest of her life as a voluntary exile and refugee in that country.

Begum Hazrat Mahal was the only leader of the 1857 rebellion to not surrender to the British. She continued to live free and on her own terms, even in voluntary exile. She died peacefully in 1879, by which time she had become a distant memory, a relic of the past. This was partly because of the destruction of all physical evidence and written records of the period during which Begum Hazrat Mahal ruled Awadh as a warrior queen. She is a part of recorded history only because of the testimony of multitudes of witnesses, her coins, and her proclamations.

Her tomb in Nepal is a neglected anonymous roadside memorial. However, her mark as a warrior queen is set in stone. She grabbed every opportunity she could, evolving from courtesan to member of the harem to a royal quasi-wife and then on to a ruling queen, even if only for a few months.

Nothing came easy to her, nor was anything given to her. Her husband and king abandoned her and her son. She seized an opportunity and filled a vacuum in leadership. She used her natural skills, talents, and the will to survive, and by her tenacity she held at bay the most powerful colonizing empire in the world. She created and led the largest army ever rallied against the British. She refused to surrender, or to conveniently, if valiantly, die in battle. Despite British efforts to erase her from history in the aftermath of the 1857 rebellion, she is venerated in Lucknow and in Awadh. She survived, as does her legacy. She won the hearts and the loyalty of the people of Awadh. They have never forgotten that she stood by them and fought with them even when their own beloved king abandoned them. It's impossible to escape her legacy when visiting Lucknow and she seems not just beloved, but still present in the city.

Through a conversation between my daughter and my mother that bridged generational gaps, I realized that no matter what else, my mother too is a survivor. She too withstood what life threw at her: war and life as a refugee in a land that never felt like her own. I see her now as the child she was and the woman she is. Whatever else she was, she lived because she survived. And that is no small feat. We might all have different journeys and come from divergent sections of society, yet no matter the challenges what matters is that we survive.

As Hazrat Mahal did.

As my mother did.

Chapter Five

Chand Bibi appeared with a veil on her head...During the night she stood by the workmen and caused the breach to be filled up to nine feet before daylight with wood, stones and carcasses.
   Abul Fazl, Mughal historian, witnessing the siege of Ahmednagar.

   Chand Bibi (1579-1590 and 1595-1600)

The queens I've written about so far were all from North India—like I am—and are familiar to me through history and legend. Venturing beyond the familiar took me out of my own comfort zone, since the northern warrior queens were part of my awareness. They were always around me even before I learned about them in school. By the time I discovered them in history books, they were already familiar to me. I grew up looking up at Lakshmi Bai's towering statues. I traveled on roads named after Hazrat Mahal and heard stories of Raziya Sultan and Begum Samru. I might not have known many details, but I knew the queens.

However, the wide regional, language and cultural divide in India meant that my knowledge of warrior queens was limited only to North India. Only when I started researching this book did I realized that there were many South Indian warrior queens, as well. Unfortunately, there is little written about these queens, so my focus inevitably fell on the most well-known of the Southern queens, Chand Bibi.

When I started delving into Chand Bibi's life and legacy, I didn't expect her to be relatable, but the more I learned about her, the more I related to her. In fact, as a middle-aged woman, I find Chand Bibi to be the queen I most identify with. She typifies the life lessons that we learn and perfect as we grow older. Less impetuous, more patient and sagacious, inclined toward compromise, but unafraid to fight.

Perhaps, if Raziya Sultan had lived to be older, she might have been like Chand Bibi. The closest North Indian counterpart was Begum Samru. However, like the other queens, Chand Bibi too was uniquely her own person. The one circumstance that sets her apart is that she held the reins of two separate kingdoms at different times of her life. She grew up in a politically unstable and charged world and she navigated her life with intelligence and integrity.

In the summer of 2012, I embarked on a journey to discover Chand Bibi and the Deccan plateau of India. The plateau comprises western and southern India, rising to one hundred meters in the north and close to one thousand meters in the south. The area covers an area that makes up eight modern Indian states. In the fifteenth century, five large kingdoms called the Deccan plateau home. Four were the Muslim-headed states of Ahmednagar, Bijapur, Berar, Golconda, and Bidar. To their south lay the huge Vijayanagar empire, the only Hindu state. The whole plateau is raised and is bordered by three mountain ranges. It fits within the triangle formed by the Indian peninsula as it pushes into the

Indian ocean to the south, the Bay of Bengal to the east, and the Arabian sea on its western side.

The best way to get to Ahmednagar is by road, so from Mumbai, I rented a car and driver and set out. The visual topography and geography of this region was as alien to me as was its history. School had informed me of the basics, but that had been decades ago, and I wasn't prepared for the reality.

The hard rolling terrain, the huge sandstone boulders, scrubby undergrowth and the reddish earth were revelations to me. We stopped for coffee at a roadside stall, where a lake sat like a jewel in a short-grassed depression.

The land fell away in a gentle slope, and purplish-gray thunderclouds shadowed mountains on the horizon. A powdery red dust coated my feet and sandals. I was forty-seven years old, getting ready to be a mother, and I felt the magical pull of this landscape as something I had never experienced before. Almost as if my senses were newborn, coming awake in an unfamiliar world.

Back in the car, I jotted in my notebook and idly flipped through some of the source material I carried with me. These are some of the facts I discovered about Chand Bibi that stuck with me.

Chand Bibi was an acknowledged leader of two different kingdoms: one, the country of her birth, the other by marriage. As a warrior queen, she not only quelled rebellions and revolts within her two kingdoms, but later took on the sheer power and might of the Mughal army. While she was not proclaimed queen of either kingdom, she was the de-facto leader of both. The cynical feminist in me sneers at this fact. In my notes I wrote, *Responsibility without acknowledgment and adulation: typical.* This may be the reason she seems so much like us, like all of us. Chand Bibi, to me, is pure inspiration.

She proved especially inspirational in the winter of 2019, some five hundred years after her death. On December 11, 2019, the right-wing government of India passed the Citizenship Amendment Act (ACA). This act amended the Citizenship Act of 1955, which provided citizenship to persecuted refugees in India, who were from Afghanistan, Bangladesh, and Pakistan. This only applied, however, to Hindus, Sikhs, Buddhists, Jains, Christians, and Parsis, but totally ignored persecuted Muslim subgroups in those countries.

Critics in India, especially its large Muslim population, worried that, in conjunction with the National Register of Citizens (NRC), the ACA would be ultimately used to render many Muslims stateless. Many people in India don't have birth certificates. This is especially true for those born before the 2000's, those who are poor, uneducated, or live in remote rural areas. If Indian Muslim citizens are unable to produce these legal documents, could they be denied their citizenship? This was not an abstract threat.

Indian Muslims in India experienced very real and visceral hatred from the right-wing Hindu nationalist ruling party the BJP, and its supporters. Students from the Muslim Jamia Millia university in Delhi protested the law on December 15, 2019. In retaliation, police stormed the campus two days later, on December 17. They entered the library and other buildings, ransacked the campus, and beat students, severely injuring about two hundred of them.

A line needed to be drawn in the sand. And that line came from ten local women who blockaded an access road, a six-lane highway near the mostly Muslim Shaheen Bagh locality.

I watched from afar as this small group swelled to a peaceful crowd of close to one hundred and fifty thousand. In the bitterly cold Delhi winters, inside flimsy tents in Shaheed Bagh, the protesters sat on the frozen ground silently protesting the ACA.

Day and night they sat, supported by an army of sympathizers. Local shopkeepers provided them with food and hot tea. Other sympathizers comprised of many religions ensured their safety and cooked and served them meals onsite.

The protestors invited Prime Minister Modi for a conversation. He never responded. Several right-wing groups threatened them with physical violence. Social media campaigns branded them anti-national elements. Media reports falsely claimed they had terrorist ties or that they were aligned with Islamic separatist groups. The Shaheen Bagh leaders consistently made statements debunking these claims and continued their peaceful sit-in protests.

As midnight December 31, 2019, became January 1, 2020, they stood and sang the Indian national anthem. This proclaimed their Indianness and was their attempt to forcefully disprove the usual fundamentalist claim that Muslims are inherently anti-Indian, anti-national, pro-Pakistan terrorist sympathizers. Their numbers grew as did their support across religious and gender divides. This stoic and steady progress reminded me of Chand Bibi. The women of Shaheen Bagh had a goal in mind, and they were unwavering in their quest. They were steadfast, patient and unrelenting, much like her.

Unlike Lakshmi Bai or Raziya Sultan, she didn't jump into battle. She negotiated, she remained patient, she tried every other strategy. This wasn't because she was afraid of a fight, which she proved by leading many successful campaigns. She simply wasn't a hot head. She always kept the future and whole picture in mind, and she remained unwilling to compromise the integrity of her mission.

Chapter Five

But she wasn't always a sagacious middle-aged woman. She started public life when she was a young girl, not yet a teenager. In 1562, twelve-year old Chand Bibi, the daughter of Hussain Shah of Ahmednagar, was married to King Ali Adil Shah of Bijapur. Like most marriages of the time, hers was a political alliance, mainly to join forces that would launch a military campaign against the Hindu Vijayanagar empire.

When Chand Bibi was fifteen, Vijayanagar was defeated by the two allied kingdoms, and its king Rama Raya was beheaded in battle. The combined forces of Bijapur and Ahmednagar then entered Vijayanagar and violently decimated the kingdom.

At this time, Chand Bibi was just another young royal woman—albeit a queen—living in luxury in the prosperous city of Bijapur. However, unlike most women of that age, she continued studying after her marriage, becoming fluent in Persian, Turkish, Urdu, and Arabic. She also didn't stay interred within the four walls of the palace and was known for riding her horse when out traveling or hunting, her face barely concealed behind a wispy veil. From a young age, she showed a steady resolution of not giving in to the mores dictating proper feminine behavior and deportment. She didn't make waves about doing what she wanted to do. She just did it.

However, she was by no means the only powerful female of that time. Many chieftains from the conquered mini states within the Vijayanagar kingdom were also women. Now that they came under the umbrella of the two Muslim kingdoms, these female chieftains demanded and achieved equality of treatment with their male counterparts.

There are theories about why Chand Bibi seemed more interested in education and learned music and horse-riding rather than merely being a royal wife and becoming a mother.

One of the most credible is that her husband Ali Adil Shah was not attracted to women, leaving his wife free to pursue her own interests.

Ali Adil Shah's early death occurred because of an unusual love triangle. He made an alliance with the King of Bidar when it was attacked by his brother-in-law Murtaza Shah, the King of Ahmednagar. In exchange for this help, Ali Adil Shah asked for an unknown and unnamed eunuch famed for his beauty, who was owned by the King of Bidar.

Distraught at being handed over like chattel, the object of his desire stabbed Ali Adil Shah to death the first time the king went to the eunuch's quarters. The punishment meted out to the murderer was swift, though its details are lost to time. I suspect the unfortunate pawn was simply not important enough to have his fate recorded by historians. Regardless, in 1579, Bijapur lost its king.

In the absence of an heir, his twenty-nine-year-old childless widow Chand Bibi got the opportunity to exert power. Of course, she was not in the line of succession, nor was she asked to be queen. Keep in mind, this was still the sixteenth century and an Indian-Muslim kingdom.

In the sixteenth century, Muslims had a home in India, but not so in the twenty-first century. Thankfully, a new type of warrior queen came on the scene to defend their rights as Muslim citizens of India. The legacy of the warrior queens has percolated into the struggles of regular Indian women. Some of these were women who protested for months against the draconian new anti-Muslim citizenship laws enacted by the reigning right-wing Hindu ruling party, the BJP mentioned above.

The protests started as a peaceful sit-in in Delhi, the capital. The protest was assumed to be temporary, which is one of the reasons the government ignored these non-confrontational protestors. But the women stayed, and the protests grew larger, with women from many other cities and states arriving to sit in solidarity with the original protestors. Even though the protest itself was peaceful there was a the very real likelihood of violent retaliations by the government at any time.

On January 4, 2020, the BBC interviewed some of the women who took part in the Shaheen Bagh protest in Delhi. Seventy-year-old Aasma Khatoon said, *"I won't leave this country, and I don't want to die proving I am Indian."*

Some women who had never spent time away from home without male escorts, spent days, weeks, even months at the protest. Eighty-year-old Bilkis, one of the oldest Muslim protestors, was listed as one of Time Magazine's *Women of the Year,* in 2020.

Back in 1579, nine-year-old Ibrahim Adil Shah II, the late king's nephew, was crowned the new sultan. This was done under the guardianship and tutelage of Chand Bibi. It is interesting to note that she was selected for this role instead of the new king's father Tahmasp, or any other male member of the royal family. A nobleman, Kamil Khan, was appointed as regent, but guardian and regent did not see eye to eye.

Chand Bibi weaponized his disrespectful attitude toward her and managed to get the regent captured and beheaded. Eventually, an Ethiopian noble Ikhlas Khan became the regent and Chand Bibi continued as guardian. However, everyone, including the new regent, knew she was the real holder of power in Bijapur. Clearly, Chand Bibi had used her fourteen years in the kingdom consolidating her power, making alliances, and gaining loyalty from the people who mattered.

The regent and guardian worked well together, which proved invaluable when Ahmednagar—ruled by Chand Bibi's own brother—and Golconda formed an alliance and attacked Bijapur. It must have seemed like a great opportunity and an easy win; a kingdom whose king was newly assassinated, ruled by a child, and assisted by a woman. The attackers could not have been more wrong.

Despite desertions from various key factions within Bijapur, Chand Bibi successfully defended the kingdom. Taking her young charge, the king, with her, Chand Bibi traveled to all the posts and rallied the troops. When the city walls were finally breached, the queen personally guarded the break and supervised the men repairing the wall. Despite the danger posed by the bombardment, she stayed there night and day during a violent thunderstorm. The young king was getting a crash course in leadership, perseverance, and victory. Bijapur prevailed, and Chand Bibi strengthened alliances to retain and regain loyalty from various other groups. The enemies stayed at the gates, however, tightening their siege of the walled city.

Despite the centuries that pass, human nature remains the same. As is so often the case today, the most irksome dangers faced by Chand Bibi came not from outside the borders of the kingdoms she led, but from within. The enemy within are invariably the most hurtful.

The stakes were equally high for the modern women of Shaheen Bagh. Their enemies too were within: the government, their own countrymen, and some sections of the media. As I read more about them and saw them being interviewed by national and international media, I saw in them shades of Chand Bibi. These mostly poor or middle-class, sheltered Muslim women. They were not royal, like the warrior queens, but they were regal and resilient. Hidden behind their hijabs and niqabs, they sat in solidarity with those affected by the ACA. The Shaheen Bagh women soon had an army of allies. Within a few days the protests grew to an area of about one kilometer.

Chand Bibi pursued the factions that had defected, then solved their conflicts and issues, winning their loyalty and fealty. A sore point among the rebellious factions was the Regent Ikhlas Khan, who was not fully accepted because of his Ethiopian heritage. He was forced to step down and Abul Hassan became the new regent. Working with him, Chand Bibi rallied an army of twenty-thousand men. She made deals with some of Bijapur's vassal states to disrupt the supply lines of the enemies at their gates.

The siege lasted a year. Eventually, the armies from both enemy states returned home, pursued and plundered all the way by Dilawar Khan, a high-ranking general in the Bijapur army. This success emboldened Dilawar Khan and on his return to Bijapur, where he engineered a successful coup. Dilawar Khan executed Ikhlas Khan and Abul Hassan and declared himself regent. He retained this post for eight years until the young king Ibrahim Adil Shah became old enough to rule.

It's interesting to me that despite the coup and her removal from power, Chand Bibi suffered no other repercussions for her rebellion. Perhaps this was because she was the queen, but royalty was never immune to assassinations and imprisonment. After she was removed from power, Chand Bibi was free to travel and live as she wished. In fact, in 1584, thirty-four-year-old Chand Bibi accompanied Ibrahim's sister to Ahmednagar. The young princess was to be married to Chand Bibi's brother, King Murtaza's son, Meeran.

There was a reason for her return to her one-time home and sometime enemy state of Ahmednagar. There are no permanent enemies or friends in statecraft, of course, only permanent interests. A power vacuum was being formed in

Ahmednagar because her brother Sultan Murtaza, clearly mentally ill, was headed toward insanity. In local colloquialism, he is still referred to as "Murtaza diwana," or Murtaza the Mad. Once, he even tried to kill his teenage son Meeran by setting his room on fire.

For the first few years back home, Chand Bibi lived under the radar. Meeran had his father assassinated and ascended the throne in 1588. His rule was marked with excesses, violence, and terror. Still a teenager, Meeran, along with a cadre of other teenagers. did whatever he wanted, He assassinated many male members of his family, anyone whom he suspected of having designs on his throne. He once killed fifteen princes in one day alone.

Fed up with his erratic and violent reign, a group of nobles organized a coup and executed Sultan Meeran. Despite this coup and the subsequent struggle for power that led to the short reigns of three kings and many wars of succession, Chand Bibi remained unaffected by the danger and intrigue swirling around her.

In this chapter, I repeatedly refer to Chand Bibi as an older and more mature women though she was just in her thirties. Unlike contemporary times, in the sixteenth century, a woman in her thirties was certainly considered older. She functioned in roles that required maturity and patience and played the role of an elder stateswoman.

In 1591, when the Mughal emperor Akbar, hundreds of miles away in Delhi, turned his eyes toward the unconquered southern kingdoms, she was forty-one. Considering the many assassinations and coups in Ahmednagar, few were more suited for leadership than her. Emperor Akbar ordered the four kingdoms to submit to the Mughal empire and become vassal states or prepare for war.

Four years later, in 1595, negotiations and king-making

came to a halt when the mighty Mughal army arrived at the gates of Ahmednagar. This was the war to end all wars for the kingdom and for Chand Bibi. This was no mere regional army but a superior fighting force that had successfully brought most of the subcontinent under the rule of the Mughal empire. In his then forty-year reign, Akbar had not lost a single conquest.

The current boy-king and his supporters fled Ahmednagar. Chand Bibi stepped into the vacuum and installed her brother's infant grandson on the throne and ruled in his stead. One of her first decisions was to rally support for defending the fort of Ahmednagar. Her erstwhile ward the king of Bijapur sent a large army, as did the kingdom of Golconda. The four kingdoms had finally realized that only by working together could they resist the Mughals.

Nehung Khan, an Ethiopian general who had once tried to rule Ahmednagar, also came to her aid. He was able to break through the ranks of the Mughal army and joined Chand Bibi in the fort. An army of thirty thousand rallied to support Chand Bibi against the aggressors. The Mughal army tried to bypass the walls of the fort by digging tunnels and lining them with explosives. Chand Bibi discovered the plan and began the task of having the explosives removed. She succeeded with two of three tunnels, but the Mughals exploded the third and broke through the walls of the fort.

While many leaders of the army prepared to flee, Chand Bibi veiled her face and headed out to fight, a naked sword in hand. The moat around the fort continued to fill with the bodies of fallen soldiers, but with Chand Bibi as their general the Ahmednagar army managed to successfully defend themselves. She then spent the entire night supervising repairs to the breached wall. By dawn, the wall had been rebuilt. The Mughal army led by the crown prince Murad was impressed with the queen. The official Mughal historians recorded her exploits.

The allied armies marched toward Ahmednagar, and the Mughal army fell short of supplies. Desperate, the Mughals struck a deal with Chand Bibi and Ahmednagar, which allowed them to install Bahadur Nizam Shah as the ruler under the suzerainty of the Mughal emperor. Ahmednagar also presented jewels and riches to the Mughals and agreed to hand over the province of Birar. These were acceptable terms because a defeat by the Mughals would have led to certain annihilation.

The Mughal army retreated to their newly acquired province of Birar, and Chand Bibi started rebuilding Ahmednagar. Much to Chand Bibi's frustration, the usual cycle of coups, power-plays, and politics quickly resurfaced. Her newly appointed chief minister, Peshwa Mohammad Khan, was someone she mistakenly trusted. Khan, her longtime ally, bypassed Chand Bibi and reached out to the Mughals with the promise to hand over the entire kingdom of Ahmednagar to them in return for royal favors.

The plot was uncovered, and Chand Bibi appointed Nehung Khan as the new Peshwa. However, the Mughal army was already mobilized and intruding into Ahmednagar. In two days, the Mughals defeated the sixty-thousand strong hastily assembled army of Ahmednagar, Bijapur, and Golconda. However, bickering within the leadership of the Mughal army prevented them from proceeding to ransack Ahmednagar. In 1599, Prince Murad died at thirty-two of complications from alcoholism.

Emperor Akbar sent another son, Prince Daniyal, with an army of eighty thousand to the Deccan. This juggernaut conquered smaller kingdoms and provinces in its march to Ahmednagar. The new Peshwa Nehung Khan clashed with

Chand Bibi and abandoned the kingdom, taking his troops with him. Chand Bibi knew that her much reduced army and the lack of a Peshwa would lead to certain defeat.

She wanted to reach out to the Mughals to propose a compromise that would consist of her handing over Ahmednagar without bloodshed while she retained rule of the city under the Mughal banner. The kingdom would remain intact, there would be no more violence, and her future and that of Ahmednagar would be assured even under Mughal rule. This made sense as the royal Mughal seat was thousands of miles away in Delhi and she gambled that life would continue as usual in Ahmednagar.

Sadly, she discussed this with one of her senior officers, a eunuch named Humeed Khan. Khan immediately spread the rumor that Chand Bibi was a traitor and was scheming to hand over Ahmednagar without a fight. Public sentiment turned against her, and a mob led by Humeed Khan entered her private apartments and murdered her. She died in 1599 at about forty-nine years of age and was buried in an unmarked grave.

In January and February of 2019, the Shaheen Bagh protestors, especially the Shaheen Bagh dadis (grandmothers), were steadfast in their quest. School kids joined the protests in the mornings before heading to school, and artists, poets, singers, and writers became permanent fixtures. Traffic issues in the capital started becoming more of an issue because of the huge scale of the protest.

The long-term sit-in became weaponized. When the Supreme Court declined efforts to forcibly shut down the protests, speculation followed that the BJP-led government allowed the protests to continue to stoke majoritarian resentments. The rhetoric went something like, *look at these Muslims creating traffic problems and going against Hindu rights.* Rumors also spread that the protest and its leaders were being paid, something that was investigated and debunked by various media channels.

Despite the challenges, Shaheen Bagh inspired similar peaceful sit-in protests across India, from the North to the Southern states. Threats of violence remained a constant, however, which included a young man who fired a gun into the crowd. The label of *jihadis* clung to the protestors.

However, ultimately, it was the Corona virus that ended the protests. By March, the virus had become a world-wide pandemic and by March 23, 2020, the protestors were forcibly removed. Some were even arrested. A few days later, the art installations and protest graffiti were dismantled, the graffiti painted over. Just like that, this months-long peaceful sit-in protest led by older Muslim women faded into history.

This ending is bitter-sweet. The CAA remains, but the protestors turned the world gaze toward their cause and forced people to reexamine what it means to be Indian, more specifically being Muslim in India. Protests and demonstrations are still springing up against the CAA as BJP-led states are spearheading campaigns to expel Muslims in their states. Just in late September of 2021, in the state of Assam, unable to prove their citizenship, eight hundred families were forcibly evicted from their homes that were then destroyed by the state security forces.

Just as the problems faced by Chand Bibi didn't disappear after her death, neither did those illuminated by the Shaheen Bagh protests. Issues are ongoing and get handed down from one generation to the next and persist through the ages. What also persists is the tradition of resistance and integrity. Being vigilant, responding to the issues of our time, and battling them to the best of our ability is our legacy: the legacy of the common people.

The Ahmednagar fort doesn't have the impressive size and scale of the North Indian citadels that sit atop cliffs or stake their claim majestically on the landscape around them. Instead, the fort sits in a slight depression and its squat, earth-bound appearance surprised me. However, despite the fort's lack of grandeur, this was one of the most impregnable fortresses in the country.

As I walked through the gates, I noted the solid structure that had held at bay some of the greatest armies of the fourteenth, fifteenth, and sixteenth centuries. The structure is compact and strong and, as I gazed upon its now rather shallow moat, I shuddered as I imagined the stacks of dead that once filled those trenches.

Inside, the grounds are almost peaceful, the gateways broad and stately, and the eighteen-meter tall and thick walls rise sharply from the flat landscape. I walked the ramparts, running my fingers across the rough surface of its dark stone bastions, in an effort to absorb the history, bloodshed, and sacrifice through my fingertips.

As I wandered the fort, I eavesdropped on other visitors. My attention sharpened as I heard someone speak of Chand Bibi's tomb. What? From everything I read and heard, after her cowardly assassination, she had been buried in an unmarked grave. I drew closer to the speaker, a local guide.

I spoke with him and learned he was taking the group to a tomb that could be Chand Bibi's tomb. I had searched for but found no historical information about where she was buried. Still, I was curious, even hopeful. Perhaps I had missed something. So, I got permission to tag along, and we set out.

A few miles outside the city, situated atop a gently sloping hill, a three-story hexagonal structure punched into the cloudless sky. I stayed on the periphery of the group, wandering in the large compound. There were two formal stone tombs in the basement tier. The bottom tier of each tomb was decorated with the ornate calligraphy of Quranic verses, their tops draped in multi-colored and embellished sheets of silk. Sticks of incense lazily swirled their strong, scented breath in the confined area. I inhaled the scent of roses.

I climbed up from the tombs onto the first platform at ground level where I caught glimpses of Ahmednagar far below. As I climbed to the second and third levels, clearer vistas of the city where Chand Bibi was born and died stretched out before me. A gentle breeze ruffled my hair, the dryness of the evening air a balmy caress.

Was she in one of those two unlabeled tombs? Who was the second person buried with her? No one—including me—can be sure if they are tombs or cenotaphs. Is Chand Bibi buried here? Is anyone buried here? How had I not read about this impressive tomb anywhere in the history of Chand Bibi? Was it merely an empty mausoleum, once intended for her but only a shell to represent an empty reality? It was peaceful here and when I think of Ahmednagar and of Chand Bibi, this air-filled structure comes to mind.

No, this is not Chand Bibi's tomb. No one knows the location of her final resting place. I learned later that the structure I visited is the tomb of Salabat Khan II and his wife. Salabat Khan was the Minister for Sultan Murtaza the Mad. Chand Bibi lies somewhere else, but that very anonymity has granted her an omnipresence in Ahmednagar. She could be anywhere. Therefore, she is, in essence, everywhere.

Most people in Ahmednagar refer to Salabat Khan II's tomb as Chand Bibi's *Mahal* (palace). No one knows exactly when his tomb became known as Chand Bibi's tomb or why. I agree with historians when they speculate that his tomb was named her burial place as a mark of respect for her heroism and courage in defense of Ahmednagar.

That is her legacy and also the legacy of the contemporary women of Shaheen Bagh. Since there was no mausoleum to commemorate Chand Babi's memory, the people of Ahmednagar commandeered one to dedicate to her. The challenges that brought about the Shaheen Bagh protests still exist and activists continue to work on the issues. Whatever the end result, the Shaheen Bagh dadis commanded the love and admiration of millions. They might never have lavish memorials built in their honor, but their legacy, like Chand Bibi's, will continue.

For like her, they are warrior queens. Just as all of us can be warrior queens.

Chapter Six

We Are...Warrior Queens

What stories do you remember from childhood? Did you recognize yourself in those stories? Did certain historical figures resonate with you or seem familiar? The answer for me is, yes. This familiarity with childhood stories is just one of many discrepancies of growing up in India. Despite the regressive beliefs of many, and the uphill battle most women face daily, seeing ourselves in our history is the gift of growing up in India.

For we have these stories of amazing women, warrior queens in whom we can see ourselves, who give us goals to strive toward. These aren't goody two shoes, demure, passive princesses. As you have seen, these stories are true historical accounts, and the main characters are fierce, exciting, complex, courageous, flawed, and colorful. These women are real people, who faced challenges, problems, successes, and failures.

These are the stories I tell my daughter, not just at

bedtime but when we're driving, chatting while walking the dog, or just cuddling. I relate them to her as tales of adventure, which just happen to have women as their central characters. She's too young to remember the difficult names. She describes them as, *"the queen who carried her baby on her back,"* or the *"the one whose daddy wanted her to be emperor,"* or the *"queen who rode on an elephant into battle."*

To her, they are as heroic and exciting as Harry Potter—her current obsession. She doesn't think that women being warriors and queens is something anomalous or out of the ordinary. They've been part of her consciousness since she was a toddler. I'm trying to create a balance. She's aware of the issues faced by rulers who happen to be women while knowing on an instinctual level that women being fierce queens and warriors isn't something outside the realm of possibility.

My daughter is a pacifist, a Gandhian who doesn't understand why violence should be the answer for anything. She references Gandhi and Martin Luther King Jr., when dealing with a bully in kindergarten. I gave her permission to hit back at anyone who hit her first, but she informed me, *"Hitting is bad. Gandhi wouldn't have hit back, would he?"* Yet she is thrilled by the warrior queens and their stories of valor, adventure, and of overcoming obstacles. To her, and to me, they are lessons in authenticity of how being a woman and a leader is neither a challenge nor an anomaly, it's just achievable reality.

What she learns from them, as do I, is that ambition is not an undesirable feminine trait. That taking what is yours is not selfishness. They show us that being a woman is not a handicap to success—if we don't let it become so. And that being mothers doesn't make us meek creatures bent on silent self-sacrifice. History teaches that, despite the presence of these warrior queens in Indian history books and even in comicbooks, they were not the norm. They existed but they were anomalous. More importantly, they were presented as footnotes of history, they didn't define history. In other words, they were presented in history as the side characters to the *real* main characters: the men. Only while writing this book did I realize how untrue this misconception is. These women were rulers and warriors in their own right, the centers of their universes just as their male counterparts were.

Lakshmi Bai was the most famous, but even she was presented as just one figure in the Indian rebellion of 1857, and not as one of the undisputed leaders and planners of the battles. Chand Bibi was written as a mere footnote in the Mughal expansion into southern India and Hazrat Mahal was designated as an uppity concubine. The strictly male perspective of history included them in the narrative *only* when they were needed to provide color, flair, or drama.

In recent years, there have been books, papers, and articles written about these women, but not nearly enough. There is a distinct dearth of sources, which makes me all the more grateful to the historians and writers who did research and write about some of these warrior queens. Far too many of these women remain tantalizing stories with no real historical authenticity behind them, which frustrates anyone seeking to learn more facts of the lesser-known warrior queens. Real scholarly research is still needed. This need is bolstered by the fact that women defined history just as men did. They are not faceless, anonymous entities. They are drivers of destiny. Just as we are drivers of destiny.

I grew up in the India of the 1980's. All through my childhood and until I turned seventeen in 1984, I lived under the complex and authoritarian rule of Indira Gandhi. Of course, she spent 1977-1980 out of power, but even then she remained a dynamic and ever-present national presence. I don't remember a single day when her name didn't appear in the newspaper or in the daily newscasts. She was a problematic yet strong leader who used the strength of her womanhood to rule. To me, a female leader was normal. She was the only leader all of India knew. Though she and her party were defeated in the 1977 elections because of the excesses of the Emergency, which curtailed civil rights and the freedom of the press, she returned to power in March 1980. Four years later, she was gunned down by two of her own bodyguards on October 31.

She was authoritarian yet charismatic, vindictive, and ruthless while commanding respect, and able to galvanize giant rallies. She appealed to the masses by cleverly invoking her gender and by aligning her image with India's martial mother goddess Durga. For some people she was Durga, warlike, strong, yet still a mother. In Indian mythology, a mother is not just a gentle nurturer but, when needed for protection, is strong, ruthless, martial, and bloodthirsty. A powerful force to be reckoned with.

I grew up with towering female images around me. From the various incarnations of the mother goddess in temples across India to the huge statues of warrior queens that dominated city squares. During the 1970's and 1980's, larger-than-life posters of Mrs. Gandhi directed the populace to only have two children per family, or to vote for her if they wanted to eradicate poverty. But there was a disconnect between living with the larger-than-life image of this strong female leader and what else I saw happening to women in India.

While there is no of lack strong female images, India was,

and still is, a traditional, misogynistic country. Physicians performing amniocentesis are not allowed to disclose the sex of the unborn child to families because of the high rates of aborted female fetuses and even more horrifically female infanticide. However, some unscrupulous doctors and other medical workers succumb to the lure of bribes, allowing female-centered violence to continue.

High levels of domestic violence, including murder, add to the tragedy of healthcare for females being a low priority for many families. Simply put, while some women die in childbirth, girls and women can also get sick and die in huge numbers because many families don't get medical care for them in a timely manner. All these factors combine to make India a country with one of the lowest male-to-female ratios in the world. According to the UN World Population Prospects 2019, in 2017, India had 48.04 females to 51.96 males. This ratio has continued in a downward trend for decades and is particularly worrying because in most of the world females naturally outnumber males. According to the same report, India is 189 out of 201 countries in terms of female to male ratio.

It is impossible to be unaware of the unescapably grim situations that grip many Indian women. But these situations aren't a simple contradiction, but a paradox. The same people who lament when a girl is born in their homes worship the pervasive powerful, even fierce, female deities. For some reason, Indians have always been able to hermetically separate these two sides of the female identity. Weak, a burden, an undesirable liability on one hand, fierce, powerful and divine on the other. Then there is that once in a lifetime woman who comes along and taps into the divine feminine and transcends all boundaries to emerge an unchallenged heroine.

India is a land of a million contradictions, and this is certainly one of them.

My journey into the warrior queens truly began when, like many of them, I became a mother through adoption. However, being a mother was only one aspect of their lives just as it is for me and for many other mothers. They were... we are, not just mothers. That's a reductive reality. The warrior queens were unapologetically female. In fact, their femaleness was front and center as part of their identities. They were leaders, their being female was almost incidental. Or perhaps they ignored this reality, something which also helped the populace—especially the men around them—to forget this inconvenient truth.

It's undeniable that all the warrior queens—typified by the fact that they were queens—were products of privilege. They were either born into or married into royalty and had the resources and power that come with that privilege. Despite their privilege, they were products of even more sexist and conservative societies than ours today. In fact, most women from royal households often had less freedom than women of a lower class. Most aristocratic women were kept in strict seclusion with no freedom to venture outside their gilded cages. They had to adhere to strict rules of protocol and moral codes with no real say in their own lives or futures. The honor of a royal house resided in its women, which resulted in profound restrictions on their movements and restricted personal decision-making powers.

Despite their high strata in society, the warrior queens were undeniably exceptional. Centuries separated them from each other, as did religion, culture, language, and the geopolitical and social circumstances of their times. Yet there are broad commonalities among them. All women—all people— can apply these as blueprints to themselves.

Each of the warrior queens had tangible goals. Goals worth fighting for. In most cases, these were fights for survival of their way of life, of conserving what was theirs for the future. Queen Lakshmi Bai, for instance, waged war to keep the kingdom for which she was steward for the actual heir, her son. Hers was a fight to the death, and she went into that fight with her eyes open.

In life, we all have something worth fighting for, something perhaps even worth dying for. For my daughter, this is animals. Since she could talk, she expressed a passion for animals. She can recite obscure facts about seahorses or manatees, snow leopards, or koalas. To her, animals are worth fighting for. In the future, she might do grander, more targeted acts than recite facts. For now, however, she understands that there are goals larger than ourselves, and that goals are important to have. Even if her goals change with time and maturity, the understanding, I hope, will remain.

The queens' goals were very specific and related to their future and ambitions. For example, Raziya Sultan wanted to rule her realm because she was her father's rightful and anointed heir. Queen Lakshmi Bai and Hazrat Mahal wanted to rule until their sons could ascend the thrones. Begum Samru wanted to retain Sardhana, rule an independent realm, and live an undisturbed life on her own terms.

I'm grateful for the abundance of female role models in my childhood. This familiarity gives me the ability to talk about them to my daughter not as figures swallowed up by history but as fierce, fearless, martial leaders, who are as much a natural part of history as any man. History obscured them, but they are ever-present in spirit, and visual reminders of them abound in street names, buildings, and statues dedicated to some of the more well-known queens.

These women's lives are as thrilling stories for any little

kid as pirates and bandits. These leaders used their femaleness and their experiences as women to achieve their goals. They made their gender—seen as weak and a liability—their strengths. They used what they had learned as women to succeed. Despite their heroic statuses in history and their privileged status, they grew up in a staunchly patriarchal world designed to thwart their success. Yet they used the skills they had learned to do what had to be done. The only power available to most women was more subtle, less in-your-face power, and could be classified as indirect power. This might be the reason they used negotiation, statecraft, and persuasion as much as they used their fighting skills.

Begum Samru, for instance, used the experiences of her life prior to gaining power to hone her skills as a dealmaker and negotiator. Raziya Sultan was able to transform her enemy and captor into not just an ally, but a husband and partner intent on helping his wife retake her throne. Chand Bibi had enough savvy to put herself in a position to be regent and military commander for not one but two kingdoms. Seizing opportunity and utilizing available resources is a valuable life lesson for any person, male or female.

Their royalty might have put them in positions of power, but their talent and determination kept them there and made them into the heroines they became. Many of them didn't succeed in their quests, and they understood the very real possibility that they could lose, given the might of their enemies. This didn't stop them from giving their all. This level of persistence and dedication to their causes drove them to reach for their goals even if they had little hope of success. The prospect of failure simply didn't get in their way.

When I delved into the world of warrior queens, I was shocked to learn just how many there had been, many more than those I wrote about. I could fill volumes of books with stories of their lives. There are tantalizing glimpses that tell us these were real women, that they existed but, as I said earlier, there isn't enough historical documentation to retell their stories in a more detailed manner.

There were two queens—mother and daughter—both called Rani Abbaka, who scored naval victories against Portuguese colonizers. This mother-daughter duo were admirals, generals, and queens. Rudrama Devi of Orugallu inherited the throne from her father but unlike Raziya Sultan, she successfully ruled for over forty years. No other contender to the throne dared go up against her. Rani Chenamma of Kittur was the first ruler to battle the British East India Company more than thirty years before Lakshmi Bai and the 1857 rebellion. There are many others largely unresearched by historians, but their stories are told in the regions of the country where they lived.

As remarkable as the queens are that I've written about, I came to realize that they are not exceptions. There is a great history and tradition of warrior queens in India. Perhaps this means that their abilities and qualities are shared by all women, maybe even all people, and we just need something worth fighting for. The most important thing the warrior queens teach us is that are no barriers that cannot be smashed through, even if that barrier is an ancient cultural misogyny that pervades society or prejudice of any kind.

Their stories are the hero's journey for girls and women. The hero's journey has been readily available for boys but not for girls.

Resistance to their leadership contained virulent misogyny, jealousy, and outright hatred. But the warrior queens simply blew past these obstacles as if they didn't exist. Perhaps they didn't. By acting as if those obstacles weren't real, they robbed the obstacles of power. Still, they didn't shy away from using the skills learned from living as women, albeit privileged women. After all, they were brilliant and knew how to exploit their womanhood to their advantage.

As I indicated earlier, my own conduit into writing about the warrior queens was adoptive motherhood. It's inevitable that adopted children deal with the trauma of being given up by their birth parents. Despite the circumstances that compelled my daughter's birth mom to seek a better life for her than she could provide, like most adopted kids, my daughter will undoubtedly deal with abandonment issues. These haven't emerged yet, but I won't be surprised when they do. What I can do is to root her in the unshakeable belief that she is important, that she belongs, that she is part of a long-standing tradition. A tradition that included mothers fighting and dying to preserve their children's rights, to ensure that they retain what was theirs.

My daughter often asks me, *"Mommy, is it true, you'll do anything for me like the queens?"*

I answer, "Yes."

In most settings, my daughter is the only adopted child and she chooses whether or not to share that fact. Still, just as there are few historical stories of the female hero, there are few stories in Western history that place adopted kids as the central character.

The warrior queens battled and negotiated on behalf of their children, their adopted children and, in fact, these children, adopted or otherwise, were often the catalysts for their campaigns.

While the trauma of early separation and feelings of abandonment for these children might never be negated, the damage can be mitigated. We can teach our children that being adopted does not mean they are second-best, nor does it mean they were easy for their birth parents to give away.

Warrior queens fought and died to protect their adopted children. Is a woman who faces the pain of giving up her child because it is in the child's best interest any less of a warrior queen? Giving up a child to ensure her safety and happiness is no less an act of love than is acceptance of that child. My child revels in the importance of adopted children to their mothers, mothers who would die and kill for them. She knows she is of paramount importance to me.

At first, I told my daughter stories of the warrior queens to highlight the fact that adopted children are as precious to their parents as a birth child. That was one of the prime reasons that this book became an idea, then a project, and eventually an obsession. Then I realized that motherhood—adoptive or otherwise—was not the only lessons to be learned from the warrior queens.

Like the rest of the world, we spent 2020 and part of 2021 in lockdown because of Covid. So as not to rely on electronic media for all our entertainment, I revived the ancient tradition of storytelling. This tradition harkened back to evenings during my childhood when frequent power cuts left us without television. If we weren't telling fictional stories, we told stories of the past, which gave the listener insight into the storyteller's personal history. Sometimes my parents told stories, sometimes one of my siblings, and most often one of the family servants kept us entertained. Anyone who was willing to tell a story found an eager listener in me.

In telling these same stories to my child, I feel as if we are both conduits through which an ancient tradition passed through to touch the future. Though I regaled my daughter with stories of the warrior queens, I realized she didn't really know that much about my life before her. This realization made me more fully appreciate how closely aligned I am with the warrior queens—and that there were ways in which she too could align with them. I wanted my daughter to know who I was as much as—or perhaps even more so—than these historical heroines. I wove in stories from my past with what I had learned through the years from these warrior queens. I related to them. I wanted her to do so, as well. I wanted her to be able to see her own stories reflected in their stories and in mine.

There was at least some aspect from each of their lives that I could relate to, despite the centuries that separated us. As I linked their various qualities to my daughter and myself, it became clear that all of us can relate in some ways to the warrior queens.

India has no monopoly on warrior queens, though there are many more of them than I first imagined. Every English schoolchild learns about Boudica in school and everyone the world knows of Cleopatra and Nefertiti. But there are a multitude of other warrior queens who have been denied their rightful place in history by those who defeated them. Hatshepsut's name was chiseled off stone tablets in a deliberate attempt to erase her from historical records. Like her, Raziya Sultan and Chand Bibi were buried in anonymous graves. It's a testament to the sheer force of these women's personalities and the power of their actions that knowledge of them survived and that they are as present in history as their many male counterparts.

There are female warriors and warrior queens across many countries and regions, from China and Japan to the cold climes of Scandinavia. There were female warrior queens in the steppes of Central Asia. There are theories that these might have been the inspiration for the myth of the Amazons. Warrior queens are ubiquitous, they are part of our consciousness and our reality. I grew up with the stories and legends of India's warrior queens, just as children elsewhere might have learned of the heroines in their own backyards. They were not background players, but interesting and inspirational characters at the center of their stories.

Yet somehow, even now, in these modern times we see them as anomalies, and very different from other women, freaks even. The idea that these women are the exception doesn't ring true when we understand just how common they are. There have been so many of these exceptional women throughout the ages and across the world, how can we possibly see them as rare personages? By distancing modern women from the legacy of warrior queens, we remove these queens as role models.

Look around. The warrior queens have always been hiding in plain sight. We have been trained to overlook their legacy and so made them footnotes. All we need to do is pause for the briefest of moments to see what has been right in front of us all along. Interestingly enough, while Information about them isn't readily available, what little remains is a testament to just how much they have to teach us. Tenacity, statecraft, ambition, integrity, dedication to courage, single-mindedness, intelligence, and practicality—and more! They are women, just like us. Just as they battle the issues of their time, we battle ours. No matter when or where they lived and died and no matter our own journeys, their light paves the way on our paths.

Warrior queens needn't be wives or mothers or even adoptive mothers. They are women of every kind. Like our sister warrior queens, how we choose to fight impacts our battles. All we need is a vision, the conviction of our beliefs, and the will to be the mistresses of our lives.

Whether snuggling or riding in the car, I tell my daughter the warrior queens' stories. I thrill in these moments, for their stories are our stories, and they must be shared.

Come, all of you—no matter gender, orientation, ethnicity or origin—join in our chant.

"Who are we?"

"We are...warrior queens."

"We are...warrior queens."

"We are...warrior queens."

Chapter Seven

"I forgive you. I forgive you for anything you did to hurt me knowingly or unknowingly. Please forgive me for anything I did to hurt you knowingly or unknowingly. I'm sorry I couldn't be the daughter you needed. And I'm sorry you weren't the mother I needed. Thank for all that you did for me with love and caring. I love you and I will miss you forever. I want you know that it's okay to leave. We'll be fine. We'll all be fine."

Just a few days before we completed the final edits on We are...Warrior Queens, I had chatted with my mother as she recovered from a stroke. Then, almost overnight, she took a drastic turn for the worse, refused food, water, and therapy, gradually sinking into a state somewhere between sleep, wakefulness, and inevitable death.

I wetted her lips with a swab, patted her forehead, and tenderly stroked her hollowed-out cheeks. I talked to her as if she could hear me and played her favorite Islamic prayers on my phone. She would have liked me to recite them to her from memory, so this was a compromise, a bridge between my respect for her deep faith and my own in-grained atheism.

Everything unresolved between us would now remain so until the end of my own life. There would be no answers, no closed loop for me, no understanding. No more recriminations. No dialogue. No way forward. This was it. The end.

Her vital signs remained strong, but by the fourth day of my vigil at her bedside she had stopped opening her eyes when I called out, "Amma, it's me." She was sinking ever deeper into a realm where I couldn't reach her. It was time. I pulled my chair closer to her side, leaned close to her ear, my face a breath away from her.

Her mouth flopped open, despite me trying to close it many times, her lips curled and drawn in over her gums. Even during the few days I had spent with her, she had shrunk into a tiny figure, fragile, crepe-like skin hanging over her slack flesh and bird-like bones. She seemed to be disappearing before my eyes. I lightly placed my hand on hers, carefully not to press down. Too firm a touch made her cry out in incoherent pain. That was her only communication. Whimpering loudly with her eyes closed tight when the blood pressure cuff tightened, when her nurse injected her IV with pain medications or flushed out the IV, when I touched her in anything beyond a caress. The end was near. For her. For us.

Perhaps there are other cultures in which this belief is common, but it certainly is in my socio-cultural, Indian-Muslim heritage. We release the dying person's soul of all burdens by forgiving and asking for forgiveness. So that's what I did. Without realizing it, tears slid down my cheeks. Grief and sadness colored by unresolved issues and a painful past is still grief and sadness. Despite everything, my mother had been the first presence in my life and had always been there. A new reality, devoid of her presence, loomed frighteningly ahead of me.

I forgave her and asked her to forgive me then I leaned

closer, kissed her forehead, and said, "Khudahafiz Amma," may God be with you. Then, with one last look, I walked out of the room. Less than twenty-four hours later, she took her final breath. I wasn't there, but my brother was. She wasn't alone, but she left alone, just as we all will eventually.

Days later, I looked through her photographs, as a baby with her new parents in Rangoon, and as that her family grew to include a total of ten children. As a newlywed bride with my father, as a mother with her own children, then, as a grandmother and, eventually, as a great-grandmother to a now almost seven-year-old granddaughter. It struck me that I could flip through her ninety-two-year long life in a matter of minutes. How very short is a human life, even one as long as hers. A blip. Less than a blip in the history of existence.

So here I am in the middle of a full circle. It's fitting, poetic even, that this is how I end this book. For We are...Warrior Queens is as much about the warrior queens as it is about my mother and my own journey to understanding her, to creating my own relationship with motherhood. I am still in shock, as it has been barely a week since her passing that I am writing this postscript.

I thought I had let go fully, but I hadn't, for the hope of a true resolution, the cruel hope of a better path forward remained. The ritual of deathbed forgiveness is not an end, it is a beginning, the initiation of a painful yet necessary process. Death is an end but it's also the first instant of an altered present and future for those left behind. Instant forgiveness and its attendant healing only happen in fiction. In real life, true forgiveness is not an end, it's a fresh start. The first step of forgiveness is an intellectual act, speaking into existence the acknowledgment of its importance. The emotional work of co-existing with the past, with its pain, its effects on personality, self-worth and identity began in that instant. I can now fully delve into the uncomfortable emotional work of forgiving my mother for her part in the shadowy, painful parts of me while also celebrating her role in the better parts of me. I have no choice but to forgive, otherwise, bitterness and anger will be the legacy I pass on to my daughter.

This is what I have learned from my fifty-five-year-old journey of being my mother's daughter. I am a warrior queen. So was she. So is my own daughter.

Flawed, imperfect, wounded warrior queens.

Reference List

Mukhoty, Ira (2017). *Heroines: Powerful Indian Women of Myth and History*. Aleph Book Company.

Kenize, M. (2008). *In the City of Gold and Silver*. Full Circle Publishing.

Katti, M. (2019). Begum Hazrat Mahal: A Revolutionary Queen. *Live History India*.

Siddiqui, F.A. (2016). *Begum Hazrat Mahal: The Unsung Heroine of the First War of Independence*. The Hindustan Times.

The Residency: Lucknow (2003). Director General Archaeological Survey of India.

Portraits of A Noble Queen: Chand Bibi in the Historical Imaginary. Deborah Hutton (2016). Marg. Pages 50-63.

Naqvi, A (2021). *Politics of Identity and Symbolism: Interpreting the Paintings of Begum Samru*. Cambridge Annual Student Archaeology Conference.

Father Patrick (1987). *Sardhana: Its Begum, Its Shrine, Its Basilica*, 3rd edition. Basilica of Our Lady of Graces.

Sharma, P. (2009). *Begum Samru: Her Life and Legacy*. Academic Excellence.

Lall, J. (1997). *Begam Samru: Fading Portrait in a Gilded Frame*. Roli Books (India).

Sharma, P. (2004). *Begum Samroo: A Play in Three Acts*. Rupa & Co.

Singh, H. (2014). *The Rani of Jhansi: Gender, History and Fable in India*. Cambridge University Press.

Rana, B.S. (2011). *Rani of Jhansi*. Diamond Books.

Sen, S. (1995). *1857*, 3rd edition. Ministry of Information & Broadcasting, Publications Division.

Dasgupta, S. (2002). *Rani Lakshmibai: The Indian Heroine*. Rupa & Co.

Pati, B. (2007). *The 1857 Rebellion*. Oxford University Press.

Jain, A.K. (1994). *The Cities of Delhi*. Management Publishing, Co.

Gupta, A.G. (2019). The Women Who Ruled India. Hatchette, India.

Brij Bhushan, J. (1990). *Sultan Rabiya, Her Life and Times*. Manohar Publications.

Gabbay, A. (2011). In Reality a Man: Sultan Iltutmush, His Daughter Raziya, and Gender Ambiguity in Thirteenth Century North India. *Journal of Persianate Studies*.

Kaur, G. (Date Unknown) *Raziya Sultan: The Great Monarch*. Punjab University.

Thapar, R.(1966). *A History of India, Volume One*. Penguin.

Scarsdale Publishing

www.scarsdalepublishing.com

www.ingramcontent.com/pod-product-compliance
Lightning Source LLC
Chambersburg PA
CBHW060526080526
44586CB00012B/641